Painting GARDEN ANIMALS with Sherry C. Nelson, MDA

40
44-5

Painting
Garden animals

with Sherry C. Nelson, MDA

NORTH LIGHT BOOKS
CINCINNATI, OHIO
www.artistsnetwork.com

WYOMING

Eleven of Wyoming's state parks or recreation areas have RV parking spaces. Hawk Springs State Recreation Area has no designated sites so the RV spaces are "open" and available on a first-come basis; no reservations are accepted. While the other ten parks do have designated sites, there are no facilities at the sites; they are "dry camping" sites. These locations accept reservations. Some of the addresses are for mail; check park for location. All the parks offer drinking water and most have dump stations. There are no shower facilities in any park. Three parks have RV size limitations (see listings). Rate group: A

Wyoming State Parks & Historic Sites
2301 Central Ave.
Cheyenne, WY 82002

Information: (800) 225- 5996 *or* (307) 777-6303
Reservations: (877) 996-7275
Internet: www.wyoparks.state.wy.us
Reservations: www.wyo-park.com

Wyoming Park Locator

Wyoming Parks

Boysen State Park

15 Ash Boysen Rt, Shoshoni, WY 82649. Phone: (307) 876-2796. Located 13 miles N of Shoshoni on Wyoming Reservoir on US 20; also accessible from US 26. 7 campgrounds, 230 sites; dump station. Fishing; boat ramp. Reservable. GPS: N 43-16.7 W 108-07.2

Buffalo Bill State Park

47 Lakeside Rd, Cody, WY 82414. Phone: (307) 587-9227. Located on Buffalo Bill Reservoir, 9 miles W of Cody on US 14. Two campgrounds, 99 sites (some pull-thru); dump station. Fishing. Boat ramp. Reservable. GPS: N 44-30.3 W 109-15.0

Connor Battlefield State Historic Site

c/o Fort Phil Kearny SHS, Story, WY 82842. Phone: (307) 684-7629. Located on the Tongue River in Ranchester in northern Wyoming, just off US 14. 20 sites. Seasonal. Fishing. GPS: N 44-54.2 W 107-10.1

Curt Gowdy State Park

13191 Hynds Lodge Rd, Cheyenne, WY 82009. Phone: (307) 632-7946. Located between Cheyenne and Laramie on WY 210, just N of I-80. 150 sites; dump station. Three lakes in park. Fishing; boat ramp (15 h.p. limit). Horse corral. Reservable. GPS: N 41-11.5 W 105-15.3

Glendo State Park

397 Glendo Park Rd, Glendo, WY 82213. Phone: (307) 735-4433. Located on North Platte River, 6 miles SE of Glendo, off I-25 exit 104. Seven campgrounds, 415 sites; dump station. Boat ramp. Marina. Reservable. Fishing. GPS: N 42-28.5 W 104-59.9

Guernsey State Park/Museum

Guernsey, WY 82214. Phone: (307) 836-2334. Located on North Platte River off US 26, 2 miles NW of Guernsey. Seven campgrounds, 24 sites; dump station. Fishing; boat ramp. Reservable. GPS: N 42-17.1 W 104-45.9

Hawk Springs State Recreation Area

c/o Guernsey State Park, Guernsey, WY 82214. Phone: (307) 836-2334. Located on Hawk Springs Reservoir in southeastern WY, off US 85, S of Torrington. 24 sites. Water available. Fishing; boat ramp. GPS: N 41-44.7 W 104-12.8

Keyhole State Park

22 Marina Rd, Moorcroft, WY 82721. Phone: (307) 756-3596. Located on Keyhole Reservoir between Moorcroft and Sundance, off I-90 exits 165 or 153/154; N to US 14 and WY 113. 170+ sites; dump station. Fishing; boat ramp. Reservable. GPS: N 44-21.8 W 104-48.5

Medicine Lodge State Archaeological/Historical Site

Hyattville, WY 82428. Phone: (307) 469-2234. Located 6 miles NE of Hyattville, off WY 31 on W slope of Big Horn Mountains. 27 sites. Horse trails. Fishing. Reservable. GPS: N 44-18.5 W 107-36.0

Seminoe State Park

Seminoe Dam Rd, Sinclair, WY 82334. Phone: (307) 320-3013. Located on North Platte River, 40 miles NE of Rawlins off I-80 exits 219 or 221. Two campgrounds, 52 sites. (Rough terrain.) Fishing; boat ramp. GPS: N 42-08.9 W 106-54.3

Sinks Canyon State Park

3079 Sinks Canyon Rd, Lander, WY 82520. Phone: (307) 332-6333. Located on the Popo Agre River, 6 miles SW of Lander on WY 131. 30 sites. 40-foot limit. Fishing. GPS: N 42-44.4 W 108-49.6

Wyoming

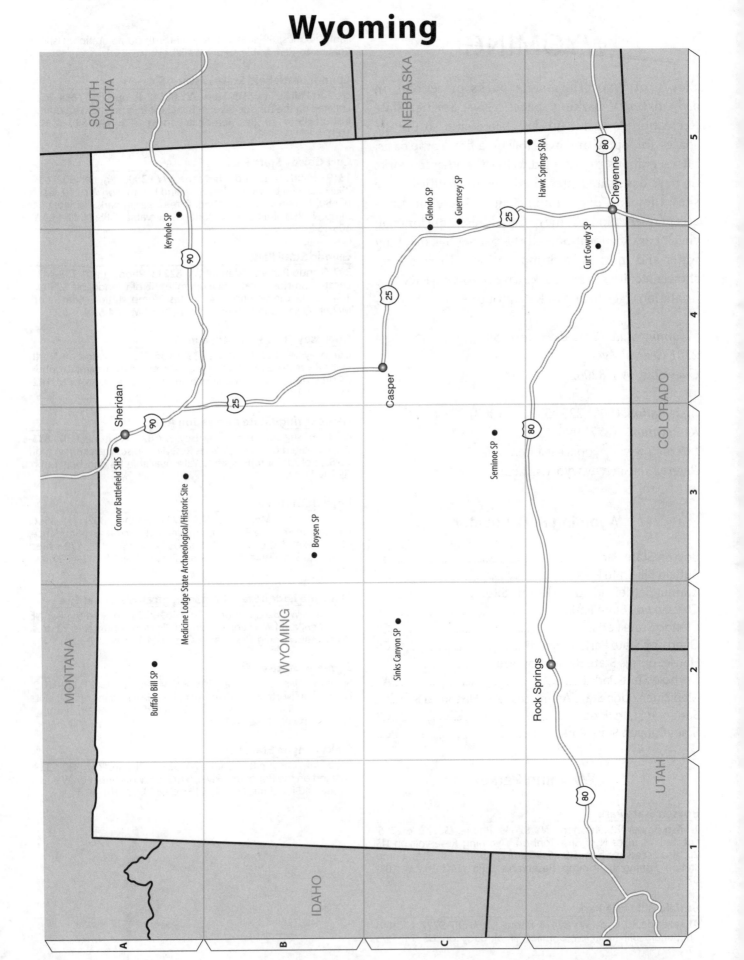

Sherry C. Nelson

Other fine North Light Books are available from your local bookstore, art supply store, or directly from the publisher.

08 07 06 05 04   5 4 3 2 1

Library of Congress Cataloging-in-Publication Data
Nelson, Sherry C.
    Painting garden animals / with Sherry C. Nelson.-- 1st ed.
        p. cm.
    Includes index.
    ISBN 1-58180-428-8 (alk. paper) --ISBN 1-58180-427-X
    1. Animals in art. 2. Painting--Technique. I. Title.

ND1380.N448 2004
751.45'432--dc22   2003058603

EDITOR: Maureen Mahany Berger
DESIGNER: Brian Roeth
PRODUCTION COORDINATOR: Kristen D. Heller

Metric Conversion Chart

TO CONVERT	TO	MULTIPLY BY
Inches	Centimeters	2.54
Centimeters	Inches	0.4
Feet	Centimeters	30.5
Centimeters	Feet	0.03
Yards	Meters	0.9
Meters	Yards	1.1
Sq. Inches	Sq. Centimeters	6.45
Sq. Centimeters	Sq. Inches	0.16
Sq. Feet	Sq. Meters	0.09
Sq. Meters	Sq. Feet	10.8
Sq. Yards	Sq. Meters	0.8
Sq. Meters	Sq. Yards	1.2
Pounds	Kilograms	0.45
Kilograms	Pounds	2.2
Ounces	Grams	28.4
Grams	Ounces	0.035

Acknowledgments

Students are the other side of the painting coin. Without the excitement and enthusiasm of the wonderful folks who buy my books and take my classes...well, there wouldn't be much point in it all. They bring me questions every day, every class. And with the answers comes more knowledge for all of us to share. I'd never be the painter I am without my students' prodding and pushing, begging for new things to paint, and maybe most importantly, telling me how much they appreciate me and how much they love what I do. As my friend and photographer Deb Galloway and I always say, "Without you, we'd just get a job at McDonalds." Thanks, ladies and gentlemen. No teacher could ask for more loving support. You're the greatest.

Terry Steele and Arthur Morris are two of the most important men in my life. They are special friends and world-class nature photographers who share their "seconds" with me. What a treasure it is seeing new creatures through their eyes. Thank you both.

Special thanks also to Ann Bunce, long-time painting friend, for your very helpful critical comments during the painting process—and for your years of friendship, too.

A last thank you to the folks at North Light Books, especially my editors. Without Kathy Kipp this book would never have been a reality. She encourages and praises, is patient and kind, a professional and a good friend too. What a pleasure to know you. Thanks also are due to Maureen Berger for your attention to every detail and for your insightful suggestions along the way. Thanks to book designer Brian Roeth, associate editor Holly Davis, and production coordinator Kristen Heller, who have had such a hand in making this book the best it can be.

Dedication

To my business partner and long-time friend, Deborah Galloway. Deb, your support and interest in my work, your skill as an organizer and researcher, and your willingness to haul camera gear around the country and across the world to take thousands of photos, from reference shots to step-by-steps for this book, have been invaluable. I could not list the countless ways in which you make it possible for me to do what I do. As they say in Norwegian, *tusen takk*—a thousand thanks!

About the Author

Sherry C. Nelson's career in painting has stretched across nearly 34 years, and has been shaped by her love of the natural world and its creatures. First and foremost she is a teacher, and has shared her wildlife painting techniques with thousands of students in every single state and many countries around the world.

If painting and teaching is her career and first love, then field work is Sherry's obsession. Travel teaching has provided her an unparalleled opportunity to see the birds and animals of the world, and to meet new students. Sherry is an accomplished and knowledgeable naturalist, and shares her love of birds and animals as well as painting with her students. She claims that field study is so addictive that it's sometimes tempting to forsake brushes for binoculars. And it's the field work that brings realism to the birds and animals she paints, endowing each species with the special characteristics that make it look real. It's easy to see that Sherry is on speaking terms with the creatures she paints.

Sherry has developed a unique approach to teaching, breaking down the instructions into a step-by-step sequence that allows almost anyone to quickly learn and easily master the techniques needed to produce beautiful and realistic animals and birds.

Sherry was born in Alton, Illinois, and received her B.A. from Southern Illinois University. The lure of the mountains of the Southwest prompted a move to New Mexico, where her children Neil and Berit were raised. Sherry now lives and paints on her 37 acres of

spectacular wilderness in the Chiricahua Mountains of southeast Arizona. Nine species of hummingbirds and the occasional black bear frequent the feeders, and coatis and gray foxes come by frequently for handouts.

Sherry's field seminars offer students the chance to find unspoiled serenity and a reprieve from workaday hassles, while learning to paint and identify the creatures which surround them.

Now, from her studio in wooded Cave Creek Canyon, Sherry invites you to join her in painting some of your favorite backyard animals.

Table of Contents

chapter one

Materials

Oil paints are easy to use and, since you'll use just a very small amount for any one project, they will last a long time. Inexpensive paints are not a savings because they are mostly oil and only a little pigment. For this book, I've used only 13 different tubes of paint, so hopefully you'll be able to buy the best quality artist's oils and thus save frustration and expense in the long run.

Always buy the best brushes you can afford. If you are a beginning painter and you attempt these projects with poor quality brushes, you may blame yourself if your paintings don't turn out right. Using good, short, bright red sables will make the techniques in this book easier to master.

If you've painted in oils before, you no doubt have many of the supplies you need. If you have not, just purchase what you need for your favorite projects from this book to minimize expense. But always start with the very best you can afford. That's your best guarantee for success.

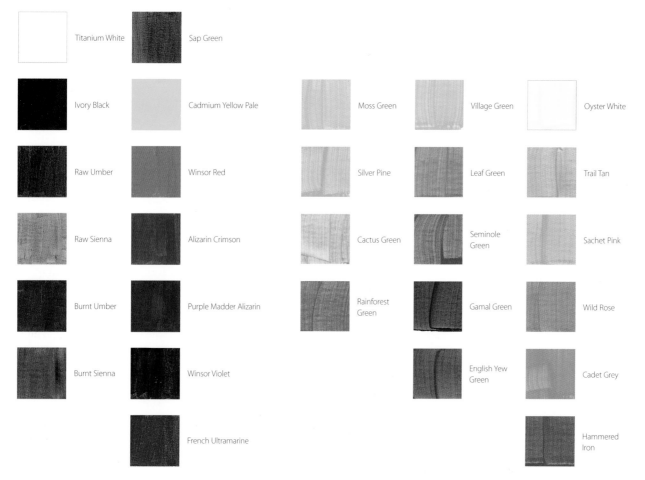

Titanium White	Sap Green
Ivory Black	Cadmium Yellow Pale
Raw Umber	Winsor Red
Raw Sienna	Alizarin Crimson
Burnt Umber	Purple Madder Alizarin
Burnt Sienna	Winsor Violet
	French Ultramarine

Moss Green	Village Green
Silver Pine	Leaf Green
Cactus Green	Seminole Green
Rainforest Green	Gamal Green
	English Yew Green

Oyster White
Trail Tan
Sachet Pink
Wild Rose
Cadet Grey
Hammered Iron

OIL COLORS USED FOR THE PROJECTS
These color samples will help you determine the oil colors you'll need for each project. The tube colors I used in this book are Winsor & Newton Artists' Oil Colours.

ACRYLIC COLORS USED TO PAINT THE BACKGROUNDS
These samples will help you match the acrylic paint colors I used in preparing the various backgrounds in the projects. The acrylics I used in this book are by Delta Ceramcoat.

Basic Supplies

Check the list of materials for each project before you begin. Purchase supplies you'll need and add to your collection gradually. Always buy the best you can afford. In the long run, quality supplies pay for themselves.

The photo above shows the basics you'll need to paint all the projects in this book. They include:

PALETTE PAD. A 9" × 12" (23cm × 30cm) strip palette for oils is best.

PALETTE KNIFE. A flat painting knife is best for mixing in drier and applying the thinned oil paint on backgrounds for antiquing.

OIL PAINTS. I used only 13 colors for all the projects in this book: Titanium White, Ivory Black, Raw Umber, Raw Sienna, Burnt Umber, Burnt Sienna, Sap Green, Cadmium Yellow Pale, Winsor Red, Alizarin Crimson, Purple Madder Alizarin, Winsor Violet and French Ultramarine.

COBALT DRIER. This product is optional, but I certainly encourage you to try it. When used as I do, your painting will be dry overnight—yet it leaves the palette workable until you are finished with the painting. Also called "drier" or "siccative."

ACRYLIC RETARDER slows the drying time of acrylic paints. I use Jo Sonja's Retarder & Antiquing Medium.

BRUSHES. Red sable short brights in sizes 0, 2, 4, 6 and 8. Also a red sable round liner brush in size 0.

ARTIST'S ODORLESS THINNER and a tiny capped jar to pour a little into when you paint. I use a small empty lip balm jar and I keep it capped until I need it.

MASONITE PANELS in the sizes suggested for each project. You can purchase large sheets and cut them yourself or have them cut at the home center or lumberyard. Use the medium-priced, $\frac{1}{8}$" (3mm) thick hardboard. Cardboard-colored is the best.

ARTIST'S GRAPHITE PAPER for transferring the designs. You'll need a sheet of dark gray and a sheet of white. Buy it at an art supply store in large sheets, not in rolls from a craft store. Craft papers may be hard to remove from the surface and may not be thinner-soluble.

TRACING PAPER. An 11" × 14" (28cm × 36cm) pad will work fine.

STYLUS. You can also use an old ballpoint pen or the end of a brush handle for marking feather lines into the wet paint.

BALLPOINT PEN (not a pencil) for transferring the designs.

PAPER TOWELS. Soft and very smooth. I like Viva the best, they will save lots of wear and tear on your brushes. Don't use the cheap, bumpy ones.

SPRAY VARNISH. Final finish for the completed paintings.

Materials for Background Preparation

If you've not painted before, you may wish to simplify the painted backgrounds in the projects and concentrate on learning the basic painting skills. Any project in this book may be painted on just a single neutral acrylic color. As you complete more projects, you may find you are ready to get a bit more colorful. When you do, just purchase some of the acrylic colors listed in the projects.

Here are the basics you'll need for preparing the backgrounds for the projects in this book:

MASONITE or hardboard panels.

SPONGE ROLLERS. I apply all background colors with these 2" (5cm) foam rollers. They give an even, slightly textured surface for painting.

ACRYLIC PAINTS. The colors for the projects in this book are Moss Green, Silver Pine, Cactus Green, Rainforest Green, Village Green, Leaf Green, Seminole Green, Gamal Green, English Yew Green, Oyster White, Trail Tan, Sachet Pink, Wild Rose, Cadet Grey and Hammered Iron.

320-GRIT WET/DRY SANDPAPER. It's black and available in packs at home centers or lumberyards.

KRYLON MATTE FINISH, #1311. A must. This acrylic matte spray will seal the surface of the background lightly, allowing the oil paints to move easily for blending.

NEWSPAPER to protect your work surface.

PAPER TOWELS. These can be the less expensive ones, since they'll just be used for clean-up.

What Sherry Uses

Compare your supplies to those I used in this book and make any substitutions as close as possible for the best results.

OIL PAINTS. Winsor & Newton Artists' Oil Colours. They are the best and are the only kind I use.

BRUSHES. Winsor & Newton Series 710 red sable short brights, sizes 0, 2, 4, 6 and 8. Winsor & Newton Series 740, no. 0 liner.

PALETTE KNIFE. I use a custom-made, flat-bladed painting knife styled after the Italian painting knives. It is the best for mixing and keeps my hand out of the paint.

COBALT DRIER by Grumbacher.

ACRYLIC PAINTS by Delta Ceramcoat.

SPRAY FINISHES. Krylon Matte Finish, #1311, and Krylon Spray Varnish, #7002, for final picture varnish.

Sometimes supplies may be difficult to find in remote areas. If you have difficulty locating what you need, you may purchase supplies by mail from:

The Magic Brush, Inc.
P.O. Box 16530
Portal, AZ 85632

Send $3.00 (U.S.) to receive a catalog, or call (520) 558-2285.

chapter two

Painting Backgrounds

Preparing the Background

Have you ever noticed the beautiful, out-of-focus backgrounds in many animal and bird photos? The animal is in sharp focus but the background, usually foliage with light and dark areas, is soft and hazy and gives special emphasis to the creature in the photo. I have adapted my background treatments to incorporate that look.

The background can make or break the look of the finished art, depending on how well it's prepared. A background should stay in the background. It shouldn't be so complex or colorful that it detracts from or competes with your subject. Simplicity and neutral colors will allow your subject to be the focal point. If your background gets too gaudy, you probably won't like the finished painting.

All the backgrounds used in this book begin first with the wet-on-wet acrylic method I'm going to demonstrate here. First, set up a work table and have everything you need nearby. You'll do a better job if you don't have to hunt for something as you work. Don't be intimidated. What's the worst-case scenario? If you hate what you get, just let it dry, sand it down and try again!

Final Finish

Not all oil paints dry with an even finish. Some, like the reds and umbers, become dull. Others look wet even when they are dry. To give the surface of a painting a uniform sheen, it is necessary to apply a final finish. The finish also protects the paint from being damaged or scratched.

When cobalt siccative is used to speed the drying time of your palette, it also shortens the time you must wait before you can apply the final varnish. The thickness of the paint you've applied to the painting also impacts the drying time. Obviously, the thicker the paint, the longer you have to wait for the paint to cure and become safe to varnish. Remember: just because the paint is dry to the touch does not mean it is ready for the final finish.

Because my painting style involves only the thinnest of paint applications, and because I live in a warm, dry climate, I probably can varnish the finished painting sooner than those of you hampered by cold weather and high humidity.

Generally, I feel safe varnishing my paintings by the second week, though I've done it sooner with no problem. I'll leave that decision to you. I use Krylon Spray Varnish #7002. It is a satin finish, oil based varnish that gives a very light, even coating and brings out the beautiful rich colors for which oils are noted. I've never experienced crazing or other varnish-related problems with this particular product.

Wet-on-Wet Acrylic Backgrounds

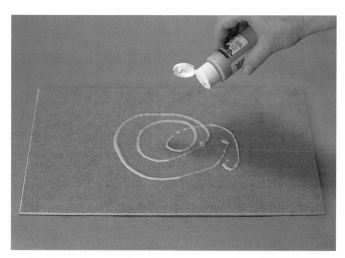

1 Begin by sanding the edges of the Masonite panel; no need to sand the painting surface. If the back is fuzzy, sand that a little too, so the particles don't get into your paint. I do the backs with an electric sander, outside.

Wet-on-wet acrylic backgrounds most often begin with a basecoat of one of the colors. Here I'm drizzling on Silver Pine, quite generously. You'll need enough to wet the roller as well as to coat the surface liberally.

How do you know when too much is too much? If the paint remains bubbly after you've coated the entire surface, you've put on a little too much. If it's sticky, and disappears right away into the surface, you've used too little.

2 Use the sponge roller in one direction until the surface is covered. Then go across in the other direction for a smoother finish. Lighten the pressure on the roller when you change directions. If you've put on too much paint, just change directions another time. The paint will gradually quit being bubbly.

3 After the first coat dries (it will no longer feel cool to the touch), sand it well. Sand the edges again and the painting surface too, to remove any dust particles that may have gotten into the paint. Press lightly with all four fingers on the sandpaper and move it around on the surface as if you were polishing it.

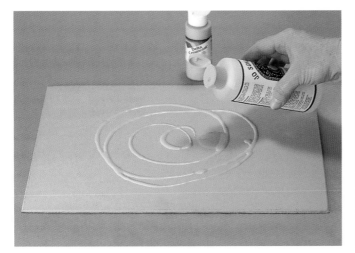

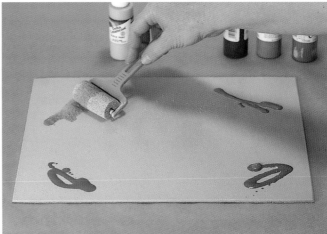

4 Now reapply the Silver Pine, using just a little less than before. Then drizzle a little puddle, perhaps half a tablespoon, of acrylic retarder onto the surface in the middle of the paint. Now, using the sponge roller, recoat the surface more quickly this time, since all other colors must be applied while the surface is still wet.

5 Now comes our first additions of shading color. Two drizzles of Seminole Green are applied on the bottom of the surface. And I've placed two matching amounts of Rainforest Green on the upper two corners of the surface. As I'm getting ready to blend, notice that I've pushed the roller lengthwise into the Rainforest Green, not across the stripe.

6 When blending, move the roller around a little, blending the edges of the new color into the background surface. If you feel you can't control the color easily, roll some off onto a paper towel or onto the newspaper. Here I've blended the Rainforest Green into the upper part of the surface, and you can see I've left the colors just a little splotchy. Remember, we want that "out-of-focus" effect here. Now I'm rolling in the Seminole Green on the bottom of the surface.

7 Here you see the Seminole Green blended into the background. The drizzles of dark color placed within it in the lower corners of the surface are Gamal Green, a shading color to strengthen the greens and give them more depth. Again, roll into the stripe of color lengthwise, not across it.

Blending and Finishing

8 The Gamal Green is almost blended now. Try to keep it within the Seminole Green area, since it is the shading color. The darker colors are hardest to control; if I need to, I can always roll off excess before blending on the line where the greens meet the blue-green background.

Were you able to get the last of the blending done before the basecoat colors dried? If so, that means you had just the right amount of acrylic retarder. If not, use a bit more next time. It is important to finish before the paint begins to dry so that the acrylic has time to "settle" onto the surface, to flatten out. If your backgrounds are too bumpy and they dry too quickly, you can simply use more paint and more retarder—and, of course, work faster!

9 With retarder, you'll need to wait overnight before sanding. Then sand well until the surface is satin smooth. Resand the edges, too.

10 Take the surface out-of-doors, preferably on a windless, warm, sunny day and spray one light, even coat of Krylon Matte Finish #1311. Hold the can about a foot from the surface and begin spraying at the top. Working from side to side, I let the spray go off the edge before starting back across in order to prevent build-up. I hold the surface to the light so I can see the spray fall, and move on as I see it beginning to coat the surface. You'll soon learn how much is too little (the oil paints won't blend easily) or too much (the oils slide around too readily). Let the surface dry outside for fifteen minutes before bringing indoors.

Additional oil antiquing is done on some of the surfaces in this book. Those instructions will be found with the project, since that glazing is done after the painting is complete.

chapter three

Transferring the Design

For each of the projects in this book, I have provided a line drawing to make it easier for you to begin painting. Because accuracy is so essential to making your animal paintings look realistic, transfer the design from a photocopy of the line drawing, not a traced copy.

If you are unable to make a photocopy of the design, you will have to trace it. Make your tracing as exact a copy as possible; every variation from the line drawing will impact the final appearance of your painting.

Use artist's graphite, sold in large sheets at art supply stores, for transferring the line drawing to the surface. It's important to use graphite that is thinner-soluble, so you can come back later and clean off the excess graphite. I'll show you how on the next page.

1 Lay a piece of dark or light graphite, whichever is specified for the project, on top of the prepared background. Lay the line drawing on top of the graphite and position it as you desire. Tape one edge of the line drawing, not the graphite paper, to the painting surface.

Now lay a piece of tracing paper over the design. Make a small mark somewhere on the design and lift the graphite to check that it leaves a mark on the painting surface and not on the back of your line drawing. Now you are ready to make the transfer.

2 Use a ballpoint pen; do not use a pencil, which tends to make wider and less accurate lines as the point wears down. Carefully transfer all detail included in the line drawing. I even transfer spots and other pattern areas so they will show through my sparse basecoat later. The tracing paper helps you determine if you have skipped any areas, and it will protect your line drawing for another use. Check the painting surface after you've drawn a few areas. Is the transfer too light or too dark? Adjust the pressure to get it just right.

Fixing & Removing Excess Graphite

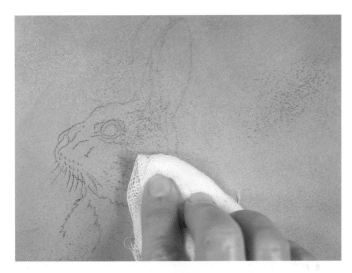

3 On very light backgrounds, or when using brand new graphite paper, the transfer is sometimes too dark. When this happens, fold a dry paper towel into a pad, and use it to rub the transfer firmly. Keep turning the paper towel to a clean side. You can pick up most, and sometimes all, the graphite this way, so be careful not to remove too much.

It particularly helps to remove excess graphite in this manner when, for example, you are painting a pale flower on a light background, when too-heavy graphite would be hard to control and white graphite would not work at all.

4 When you've completed the design and the paint is dry, you can remove any excess graphite that still shows around design edges. Dip a large bright brush (I use a no. 8 because of the firmness of the bristles) into odorless thinner. Blot the brush on a paper towel. Pull the brush along the edge to lift up the graphite line. You can see from this example that it is very important to have graphite that is thinner-soluble.

Remember I spoke of doing very complete transfers, including all pattern detail? With thinner-soluble graphite, you never have to worry about removing graphite lines that could show underneath your sparse basecoats; they simply dissolve into the paint as you blend, in a way that water-soluble graphite, made for use with acrylics, won't do.

A brush dampened with thinner can also be used like an eraser as you are painting. You can lift out small areas of paint, clean up along edges and remove mistakes entirely, if need be. Just remember to dip, then blot. If you leave thinner in the brush, it will bleed out into the painting as soon as the brush touches the surface.

chapter four

Setting Up the Palette

Not all disposable palettes are equal. I prefer a 9" × 12" (23cm × 30cm) size; it is easier to work from and takes up less space than the larger sizes more appropriate for large canvas work. Make sure the palette you buy is oil-impervious. If you put out paint and an hour later discover an oil ring around each color, the palette is *not* impervious to oil and will ruin your paints by absorbing most of the oil out of them.

You'll also have the choice between a wax and a matte surface. Each has its own benefits, and either will do a good job.

Do not tear off a single sheet to put the paint on. Leave the sheets attached to the palette so the whole thing doesn't slide around as you work. If you must use a single sheet, such as in a class, tape it in a comfortable position on your painting table so you don't have to hold it down while you load your brush.

Fold two or three paper towels in quarters and stack the folded ends under the edge of the palette pad. That way you'll have a flat surface to dry-wipe the brush on, folds to slide the brush between to squeeze dry, and the palette will hold them down so you don't have to handle them or have them in your way. If you are right handed, put the whole arrangement on your right. These are small details, but taking care of them up front will save lots of time for the real fun to come.

How to Keep your Palette Fresh

If you must stop painting for a while, cover the palette to reduce exposure to air. Since cobalt drier is an oxidizer (drying the paint on contact with the air) the more airtight you can keep the palette, the longer you can extend the life of the paint. A palette keeper with a tight fitting lid for the 9" x 12" (23cm x 30cm) palette is something you may want to invest in.

The paint will dry more quickly on exposure to heat, so keeping the palette cool will preserve it. Conversely, if you want your painting to dry more quickly, keep it warm.

If you cannot finish your painting within a day or two, simply toss out the old paint and put out fresh, since the drier eventually makes the palette unworkable. If you store the palette in a palette keeper, keep it cool, and do not use drier, the paint will stay workable almost indefinitely.

Preparing the Palette

1 Here's how I lay out my paint. I've found that a quarter-inch (6mm) of paint from the tube of each color is plenty. I lay the colors out in two rows: the most-used black, white and earth colors in the bottom row, closest to me, and the reds, greens and yellows in the top row, furthest from my hand.

Leave space between them for mixing the drier into the paint, and for making loading zones and mixes around the different colors.

2 Dip the palette knife into the drier and bleed the excess off the knife on the side of the bottle. Immediately recap the bottle to keep it from drying out. Now, with this small amount—less than a drop—of drier on the knife, tap the knifepoint next to each patty of paint. The spot of drier should be the size of a freckle, no more. If your palette is waxed, the drier will bleed out a bit; it won't on a matte surface. Use only this tiny amount and *no more*. You want the palette to stay workable for many hours and yet, with the sparse amounts of paint we apply, have the painting dry overnight.

3 Now, mix in the drier. Work it into the paint thoroughly, right away, before it dries on the palette. Notice how after mixing it in, I scrape the paint up into a tight pile. That leaves less surface area exposed to drying and extends the life of the paint on the palette even more. Wipe the palette knife thoroughly between colors.

4 Here's how your palette should look when you're ready to paint.

chapter five

Loading the Brush and Mixing Colors

A painting surface has a certain amount of tooth and will hold only so much paint. Any excess oil paint you apply over and above that simply slides around, mixing with other colors and making what oil painters refer to as "mud." Mud comes from getting too much paint on the brush and transferring it too heavily to the surface.

Animals are very detailed creatures. If you apply the base hair color too thickly, all the surface detail of individual hairs will simply blend into the basecoat and disappear.

Painting realistic animals and birds in oils means learning to paint with sparse, small amounts of paint so you have maximum control over the detail you will be putting on top. Notice in the photos in this book that I have little if any paint visible on the brush. I load one side only with only a small amount of dry paint. Dry paint on a dry brush results in good control.

The best way to control the amount of paint you pick up is by loading your brush from "loading zones," which I'll show you on the next page.

Using a "Dirty" Brush

It's so unusual for me to wash the paint out of a brush, that when it *is* necessary, the instructions in the projects will say so.

Washing out the brush removes the dirty color, which is just what you need to help tone and control the strong intensities in your painting. If you pick up clean color at every step, you will have a much more difficult time keeping your colors compatible and controlled.

Keep the lid on the thinner and your flat brushes out of it for the most part. We'll use thinner mostly with the round brush to extend the oils for some detail work on guard hairs and whiskers. Round brushes are longer and more flexible; the paint must be thin for the brush to be able to control its application.

The "Loading Zone"

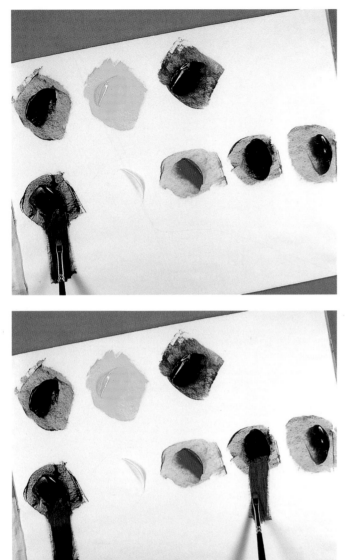

1 This is what a loading zone looks like. I've picked up just a tad of black paint, and pulled it into a strip of sparse color using a no. 4 bright. Work the paint until the loading zone is flat and dry and the paint is evenly distributed. The purpose of the loading zone, remember, is to reduce the amount of paint you pick up. You don't want any excess in it. The best way to tell if you've got the right amount of paint is to check the surface: the main patty of paint should be shiny; the loading zone should have a dry, matte look.

You can usually pick up enough paint from a dry loading zone for 8 or 10 applications of paint before the area becomes too dry. Then go up to the patty and pull down just a smidgen of paint to "feed" the loading zone once again. Distribute the fresh paint throughout and you're ready to go. But don't add more paint until you just can't get any more paint off the brush onto the painting surface.

The process of creating a loading zone puts excess paint in the brush. Always dry-wipe the brush on paper towels and reload before going to your painting surface.

2 Here I'm making a second loading zone at the edge of the Raw Umber so that I can make a mix of the Ivory Black and Raw Umber, very commonly used on many animals and birds. The second loading zone is made the same as before. Squeeze the brush dry to remove excess paint after you've made the loading zone.

To make the mix, pull the brush down the Raw Umber loading zone, then down the Black, then back to the Umber, then back to the Black. Now you've created a mix of the two colors. If you desire a browner mix, load last in the Raw Umber loading zone. If it's a blacker mix you need, load last in the Black. Whichever color you load last in, will be the dominant color on the brush.

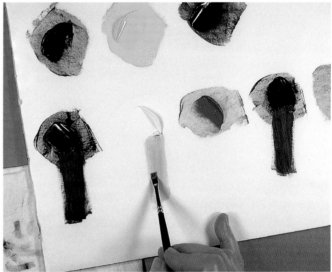

3 Ivory Black + Raw Umber is used for the basecoat of some of the fur areas. When you've done that step, slide the brush between folds of the paper towels and wipe dry. With this dirty brush, make a Titanium White loading zone. Pull the paint out as before and work the color until it's evenly distributed throughout the loading zone. The dirty color in the brush makes the White a grayed value, which is perfect for most applications. Normally you don't want the first light value you add to be pure white. Many of the first highlights on an animal's fur or on a bird's feather lines—and the lowlight values which underlay highlights—all come from the "dirty brush" + White loading zones you see here.

4 When you're ready for final highlights, squeeze the brush to remove excess paint and make a new loading zone to the side of the old one. This time, since you had dirty white on the brush instead of the dark mix, the white zone stays much whiter for those strong highlights. White is a very heavy, opaque color. Be sure to pull just the bare minimum into the loading zone so you keep control of how much you pick up and carry to the painting surface.

5 Since white is very strong, you may need to remove it from your brush before reloading in dark mixes, or moving to a translucent color such as Raw Sienna. Wash it out? No need. Instead, go to the edge of the Raw Sienna patty and work a little into the brush. Then wipe that color out of the brush taking the white with it. In essence, you've cleaned your brush with the new color.

6 Now you're free to make a Raw Sienna loading zone without worrying that the white might dilute it.

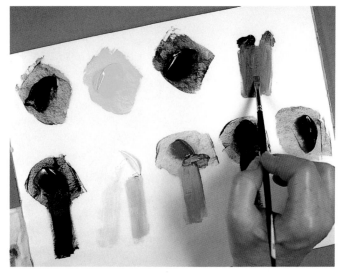

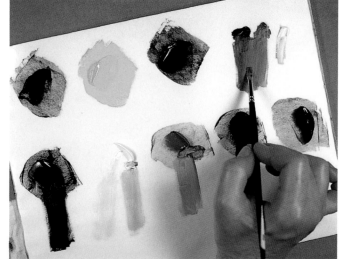

7 Sometimes it's easier to take some paint to another part of the palette to facilitate mixing. Here I've picked up a little glob of Raw Sienna on my brush and carried it to an unused area. Then I moved a little Sap Green over beside it. Now I'm making a "double" loading zone, pulling a little of each color down until I have a fairly even mix of the two. When you need to load repeatedly in the same or a similar mix, this is often an efficient way of doing it. Plus you can make instant color adjustments by adding a bit more of one hue or the other.

8 Now I've taken a bit of white and placed it next to the Raw Sienna + Sap Green mix. I'll gradually add a brush load of the White at a time to the green mix to lighten it. This is my favorite mix for the light value of leaves and other greenery, and I find making the mix in another area on the palette speeds up the process.

In addition, once I get the greens mixed to suit me, I don't have to worry about them being in the way of other mixes I might want to make next to those patties of color.

9 Thinning paint for whiskers, guard hairs and other details is very easy. Pick up a little bit of the desired color on the round brush and move it away from the loading zone. Now dip the round brush into the thinner to pick up a drop or two and brush-mix the thinner into the paint. A little of the mix will suffice, so this is an efficient method of making just what you need and no more.

Thinner evaporates very quickly. You may need to add a bit more thinner if you are working out of the puddle for very long. And the paint should be ink-like in consistency for the round brush to handle it well. If your animal's whiskers are too heavy and the paint breaks into fuzzy lines, you simply need to add more thinner to the mix so the paint will flow off the brush into perfect fine lines. A little practice wouldn't hurt either.

chapter six

The Essentials About Animal Fur

Hair. Fur. Here's what Webster has to say: Hairs are the individual, cylindrical, often pigmented filaments that cover an animal's body. Fur is a thick coat made up of an undercoat of dense, thick hair, covered by coarse hairs, called guard hairs.

An animal's coat is adapted in many ways to protect it from the sun's rays, wind, and freezing temperatures. To do that job, the hairs are waterproofed by sebum, an oily secretion of glands that are associated with the roots of the hairs. The color in hair is created by the presence of melanin.

Often the guard hairs, the outer layer of longer, more bristle-like hairs, make a tough covering for the densely packed underfur. In younger animals, the guard hairs are not fully developed, and you see the undercoat of dense hair more readily, with a few sparse guard hairs extending beyond it.

This coat sample is typical of many animals.

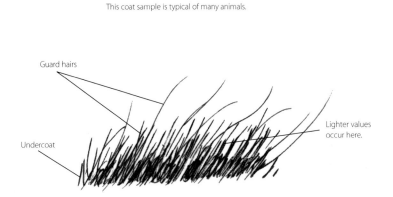

Guard hairs

Undercoat

Lighter values occur here.

Notice that there are many fewer guard hairs than undercoat hairs. Only some of the guard hairs will be painted in detail.

Reference Photos / A Guide to Fur

Young animals don't have a full coat yet. This kitten has a dense undercoat, but almost no guard hairs. Notice the few long hairs that stick out at the edges of the body.

PHOTO: DEBORAH A. GALLOWAY

This beautiful gray fox has a combination coat of agouti (or ticked) fur along with the dramatic solid color white and rufous areas. Look at the tail: it's like a plume. This photo was taken in cold weather and the hairs are standing out from the tail to trap an insulating layer of air.

PHOTO: DEBORAH A. GALLOWAY

This pup is not so much "hairy" as he is plush. That's the dense undercoat, not yet covered with adult hair. Remember when painting fur: all fur does not consist of individually visible hairs!

PHOTO: DEBORAH A. GALLOWAY

This dog's head and ears are black. Note the variation of values within the black caused by the contours of the animal's body underneath.

PHOTO: DEBORAH A. GALLOWAY

Here's an example of the agouti coat combined with a solid rufous area. This is our local Apache Fox Squirrel.

PHOTO: DEBORAH A. GALLOWAY

Agouti or "Ticked" hair

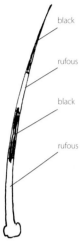

black

rufous

black

rufous

Here's how a typical
ticked hair looks
from the side. It's
easy to see from this
sketch what a var-
ied coat this unpat-
terned ticking pro-
duces.

The wild cottontails have ticked coats also, but they are
much softer to the touch and the coat is more irregular.
This is a good example of how hair does *not* always follow
the body shape, and how it varies so
much in length on most animals.

PHOTO: DEBORAH A. GALLOWAY

Many animals have straight hairs, and when the body
curves, the hairs do not curve with it. This cat's plush,
dense coat also shows lovely value variations within it.

PHOTO: DEBORAH A. GALLOWAY

This gorgeous Maine
coon cat displays the
type of long, loose, dra-
matic hair for which it
is known. Notice the
hair clumps a bit into
larger sections rather
than laying in individ-
ual hairs. The coat
also flexes differently
due to its length,
exhibiting many dif-
ferent growth direc-
tions.

PHOTO: LAURA NORDIN

Here's a fully adult mountain lion with the short tight coat that is
typical. The hairs follow the shape of the body contours closely, but
are so dense they still seem plush rather than appearing as individual
hairs.

PHOTO: DEBORAH A. GALLOWAY

Fur Facts

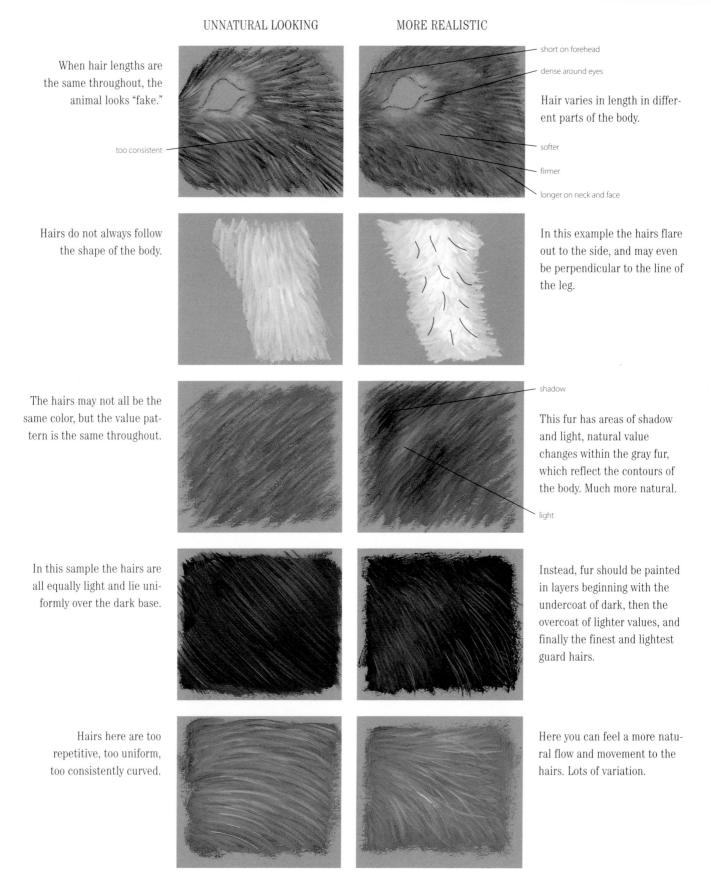

UNNATURAL LOOKING   MORE REALISTIC

When hair lengths are the same throughout, the animal looks "fake."

too consistent

short on forehead

dense around eyes

Hair varies in length in different parts of the body.

softer

firmer

longer on neck and face

Hairs do not always follow the shape of the body.

In this example the hairs flare out to the side, and may even be perpendicular to the line of the leg.

The hairs may not all be the same color, but the value pattern is the same throughout.

shadow

light

This fur has areas of shadow and light, natural value changes within the gray fur, which reflect the contours of the body. Much more natural.

In this sample the hairs are all equally light and lie uniformly over the dark base.

Instead, fur should be painted in layers beginning with the undercoat of dark, then the overcoat of lighter values, and finally the finest and lightest guard hairs.

Hairs here are too repetitive, too uniform, too consistently curved.

Here you can feel a more natural flow and movement to the hairs. Lots of variation.

Painting Coat Types Step by Step

	STEP 1	STEP 2	STEP 3

Solid color fur:

Apply dark value.   Add lighter values; connect values with blending.   Highlight with lightest values. Add longest guard hairs.

Agouti or "ticked":

Dark pattern of undercoat varies in value.   Light pattern of overcoat varies in value too.   Guard hairs—just a few.

Combination of agouti and solid color:

Colors for undercoat separate at first.   Agouti and solid colors connected with short strokes where they meet.   Overcoat of light on agouti, plus a few guard hairs.

Long, loose hairs:

Undercoat.   First light value.   Final hair strokes.

Short, straight hair:

Undercoat in several colors.   Blend between colors; strengthen dark.   Blend between values; add light guard hairs.

Black Bear Cub and Pygmy Nuthatch

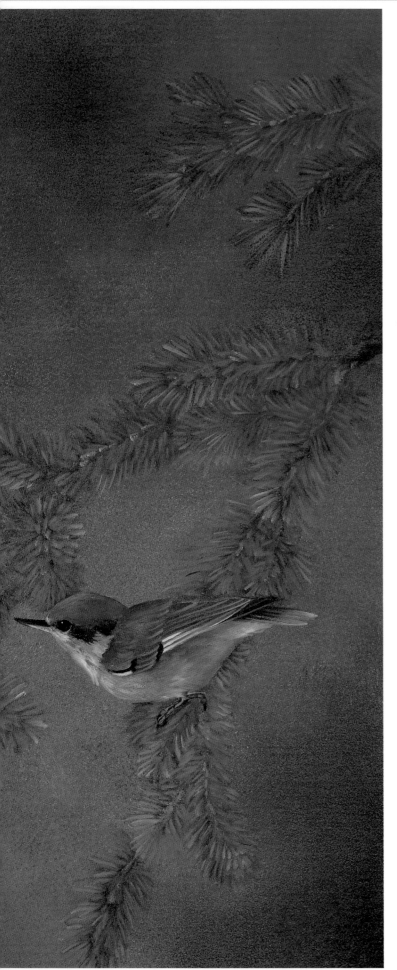

*H*ave you ever thought about how amazing it would be to have bears in your garden? I can well remember the jolt of surprise I felt the first time I looked out at the bird feeder to see a great black critter downing sunflower seeds for an early-morning snack. We've had many black bears in the yard since and have learned to live with them absconding with hummer feeders and making off with suet blocks.

Wild creatures often interact in interesting and varied ways. In my painting, this nosy cub is taking notice of a high-elevation inhabitant, the active, busy little nuthatch. Perhaps the bear cub has learned from his winged neighbors just how good seeds and nuts can be!

Color Mixes

Use these swatches when mixing oils or matching to other paint mediums.

White + Raw Umber + Black

Raw Sienna + Raw Umber

Burnt Sienna + Raw Sienna

Raw Umber + White

Black + Raw Umber + White

White + Raw Sienna

Black + Raw Umber

White + Raw Umber

Black + Raw Umber + White

Black + Sap Green

White + Sap Green

Raw Sienna + White

Black + White

Line Drawing

Transfer this line drawing to the prepared background using white graphite paper. Be very accurate when transferring eyes, facial features and the wing and feather areas on the bird. Don't let fur "grow" outside the drawing.

This pattern may be hand-traced or photocopied for personal use only. Enlarge at 147% to bring it up to full size.

To paint the background, you'll need:

- Hardboard (Masonite) panel, 14" x 11" x ⅛"
  (36cm x 28cm x 3mm)
- Sponge roller
- Acrylic paints by Delta Ceramcoat
  Gamal Green
  Rainforest Green
  Cactus Green
- Paper towels
- Protected work surface
- 320-grit wet/dry sandpaper
- Krylon Matte Finish no. 1311
- Disposable palette for oils
- Palette knife
- Odorless thinner
- Cobalt drier (optional)
- Oil Paints
  Ivory Black
  Sap Green
- Cheesecloth

To paint the Bear Cub and Pygmy Nuthatch, you'll need:

- Oil paints
  Ivory Black
  Titanium White
  Raw Sienna
  Raw Umber
  Burnt Sienna
  Sap Green
- Brushes
  nos. 0, 2, 4, 6 and 8 red sable short brights
  no. 0 red sable liner
- Odorless thinner
- Cobalt drier (optional)
- Palette knife
- Paper towels
- Disposable palette for oils
- White graphite paper
- Tracing paper
- Ballpoint pen
- Stylus
- Cheesecloth

This photo shows a branch from a Colorado Spruce, the tree I picked for the bird's perch in the painting. You can see that I chose to simplify the branch, keeping the graceful structure, but eliminating many of the smaller branches for simplicity.

PHOTO BY DEBORAH A. GALLOWAY

These pictures give some insight into the active, busy lifestyle of a Pygmy Nuthatch. A tiny bird, this is one that bounces from branch to branch—and might well take a curious, eye-to-eye look at a black bear cub.

PHOTOS BY TERRY R. STEELE

This is a mounted black bear cub about six months old. No matter how good, a museum mount never offers as much information as a photo of a live animal. However, I found it useful as a guide to the basic form of the cub, particularly the head features, which never show up well in photos taken in the wild. I then studied photos of younger cubs, and included some of those unique characteristics in the finished painting.

PHOTO BY DEBORAH A. GALLOWAY

Pygmy Nuthatch

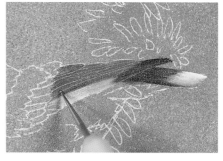

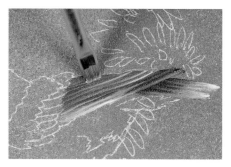

1 Review chapter 2, Painting Backgrounds, before beginning. Basecoat the Masonite panel with Rainforest Green, using a sponge roller. Let dry, and then sand. Recoat the central area of the surface with Rainforest Green, rolling smoothly. Then drizzle Gamal Green around the edges of the surface and blend into the Rainforest Green. Finally, drizzle a little Cactus Green into the central area of the surface to create highlight areas, and blend this into the surrounding colors.

Let the panel dry, sand lightly, and spray with a matte finishing spray. Let dry overnight and then transfer the design.

2 These feather areas can be done with a no. 2 or 4 bright. Base the dark value on the bird's tail using a dark value mix of Black + Raw Umber. Base the remainder of the tail with White + Raw Umber. Base the tips of the long primary wing feathers with the dark tail mix. Base the medium gray feathers with Black + Raw Umber + White, drawing in stylus lines as a guide to the feather lines as shown. Base the lower part of the primaries with White + Raw Umber + Black.

3 Use the chisel edge to blend between values on the tail. Add fine lines with a dirty brush + White, using the chisel edge of the bright. Paint fine, dirty-brush + White feather lines on top of the stylus lines in the wing area. Use a cleaner White for the lines on top of the lightest value feathers so they show up.

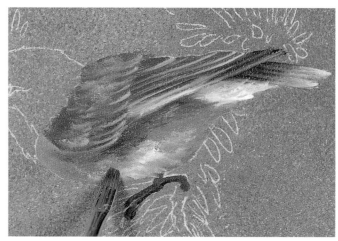

4 Base the lower portion of the wing coverts with Raw Umber and draw feather lines into the wet paint using a stylus. Base the remaining wing coverts and the shoulder of the bird with a medium gray mix of Black + Raw Umber + White. Base the breast area with White + Raw Umber + Black.

5 Using the chisel edge of a no. 2 bright, add the feather lines on the wing coverts using a dirty brush + White. Apply white highlights on the shoulder to indicate rough feather shapes. Shade next to the wing on the breast using Black + Raw Umber. Add highlights with White. Base the bird's legs with Black + Raw Umber.

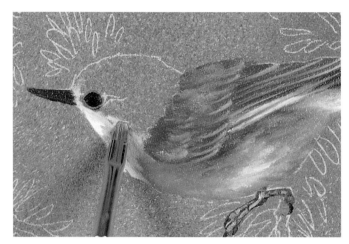

6 Blend the highlights on the shoulder to soften. Blend the shading and highlights on the bird's breast, following the growth direction of the feathers. Rehighlight with additional White if needed. Accent the upper breast with just a little Raw Sienna.

Using a no. 0 bright, add a dirty white line of highlight down the center shaft of the leg, and on each toe. Soften a little into the basecoat. Thin a little Black with odorless thinner and add leg lines and toenails, using the liner brush.

Base the eye-ring with Raw Sienna, using a liner. Wash out the liner with odorless thinner, dry the brush on a paper towel and load the tip with clean Black. Fill in the eye very carefully, maintaining a clean edge. Base the beak with Black + Raw Umber. Base the throat with Raw Sienna + White.

7 Using the chisel edge of a small bright, highlight the beak with a line of dirty white. Add a highlight dot in the eye using clean White on the liner brush.

Using a no. 0 bright or no. 0 liner, place the eyeline of Black + Raw Umber in front of and behind the eye, narrowing the eye-ring with the mix where the colors meet.

Base above the beak on the forehead with White. Base the forehead with Raw Sienna + Raw Umber. Base the nape of the neck with a gray mix of Black + Raw Umber + White.

Detail the throat with tiny feather-shaped strokes of Raw Sienna. At the edge of the throat, add a shadow of Black + Raw Umber.

8 Highlight the forehead and nape with short strokes of dirty white. Shade behind the eyeline onto the nape with additional Black + Raw Umber.

9 These steps may be done now, or on a dry surface.
Detail the lower portion of the beak with a White highlight.

Add the small black and white feathers at the edge of the wing where shown. Rehighlight the feather lines on the lightest primary wing feathers.

Accent the lower breast and under the tail coverts with Raw Sienna + White.

Spruce Branches

10 Base the dark areas on the branches with Raw Umber. Base the light value with Burnt Sienna + Raw Sienna. Roughly base the needle masses with the chisel edge of a no. 2 or 4 bright, using Sap Green + Black.

11 Lift out needle shapes using a small bright dipped in odorless thinner, then blotted on a paper towel. Do a few, then redip the brush in thinner, reblot on the paper towel and lift a few more. Continue this process until the shapes and forms of needle clusters have been developed.

12 Now add additional needles to each cluster using Sap Green + White. Make some lighter than others, some shorter, and so forth, varying them to create a natural look for each branch. Allow some to come over portions of the reddish branch areas, as they naturally would. Finally, highlight just a bit of the remaining visible branches with Raw Sienna + White.

Black Bear Cub

Eye-ring color is very dark. It only appears lighter against the black.

Underlying fur appears choppy, thick—not hairy.

13 Outline the cub's eyes roughly with a very dark mix of Raw Umber + White. Use a clean brush to fill in the eyes with pure Black. Base around the eyes with Black + Raw Umber, narrowing the eye-rings as shown.

Base the nostrils with clean Black, and base the remainder of the nosepad, nose, and mouth opening with Black + Raw Umber + just a speck of White, so the mix is very dark. Begin to apply highlights on the nosepad and mouth with a dirty brush + just a little White. The value should be just a bit lighter than the basecoat.

14 Highlight the eyes with White, using a no. 0 bright. Smudge the eye-ring into the surrounding dark areas with a dry brush. Break at the eye corners with additional Black to recess the eye farther into the face. Blend highlights on the dark nosepad and mouth areas. Then add a bit lighter value of White at the top of the nosepad and at the inner edges of the nostrils. Blend to achieve a little texture. Base the muzzle next to the nose and mouth with Raw Sienna + Burnt Sienna. Base the rest of the area above the nose with Raw Sienna + Raw Umber. Base the area below the left eye with Raw Sienna. Base the remainder of the muzzle with a yellowish mix of Raw Sienna + White. Use a no. 4 bright to chop on colors following the hair's natural growth directions.

Notice how growth direction of hairs on face give shape and dimension.

Areas of lighter value should be placed with growth direction.

Chop on areas of dirty white to give dimension. Place all first, then blend to soften (see finished art on page 28).

15 Using a dry chisel edge, blend between values on the face, chopping the brush to suggest hair-like lines. Vary stroke length to conform to hair length differences. On the chin, for example, the hairs are very short; on the forehead and sides of the face, they are longer. Light muzzle colors must also be blended into the dark areas around the eyes. Don't leave hard lines between light and dark areas; they will make your bear appear masked. Now add additional highlights of White + Raw Sienna, chopping the color loosely to make it look like fuzz. Finally, thin the light mix slightly and use the liner brush to add fine chin hairs along the muzzle edge.

16 Using the no. 8 bright, lay in all the remaining dark areas of fur with Black + Raw Umber. Outline the right ear with Raw Umber + White. Lay in some rough fluffy areas of Burnt Sienna + Raw Sienna inside the ears. As you work, establish hair growth direction with the chisel, fluffing and pulling strokes a little.

Dimension and depth are added with Black + Raw Umber + White strokes, chopped in the direction of growth, using a no. 4 or no. 6 bright. Note that the top of the head, the edge of the left ear and the sides of the face, cheek and neck are all given some form with these additions of dark gray.

Black Bear Cub, CONTINUED

17 With a dry brush, blend the edges of the dirty white areas following the direction of growth and the length of the hair. Soften the lights enough that they become part of the natural value changes of the hair, but don't blend them in so much that they muddy the fur. Soften the darks into the light values of the forehead.

Chop and blend the ear hairs a little, creating a fluffy look.

Using a smaller bright, such as the no. 4, begin to pull hairs out just a little from the edges of the body to break up the outline and to make the cub look fluffy, as bears do when they are young. Ask yourself at this point: Does the cub need more light in the fur? If so, add additional Black + White for final highlighting.

18 Now that the side of the face is nearing completion, you can go back to the slightly thinned Raw Sienna + White mix and pull the final chin hairs along the edge of the jaw using the round brush. Some of these will be pulled out over the dark fur of the neck below.

Highlight the reddish areas inside the ears with finer, individual hairs of Raw Sienna + White, using the liner brush.

Thin a bit of the dark fur mix (Black + Raw Umber) and, using the liner, begin to do the final guard hairs, the baby fluff that gives this animal a younger look. These hairs can be pulled in many directions, as you see here, for a random, soft look. Every edge of the head and neck should be broken up with some of this detail.

At the bottom of the neck, I softened some of the hairs into the background using cheesecloth. This adds depth and gives a base for the hair I added on top.

19 Finally, here's how the bear cub looks with "every hair in place."

20 When the painting dries, spray it very lightly with a matte finish spray to protect the still-tender surface.

Then some very dark green glaze may be added around the edges of the surface to suggest that the bear cub and nuthatch are surrounded by forest. I used Sap Green + Black, thinned it slightly with odorless thinner and added a drop of cobalt drier to the mix for speedier drying. I placed the glaze on the surface in thin scrapes of color applied with the palette knife.

You can see the unblended splotches here, along with those on the lower left of the surface, which have been softened into the background with cheesecloth.

Oil paint antiquing gives a richness to an acrylic background that can be obtained no other way. And a great advantage is this: If you don't like what you've done, you can simply remove the glaze with a little odorless thinner and a paper towel.

Chipmunk and Chickadee

We were visiting our dear friend Ruth at her cottage in Minnesota—relaxing on a deck that overlooks the lake. Just a few feet away stood this lovely weathered feeder. The little chipmunk came out of nowhere, up the post and into the seed—smug with his own cleverness. Out came the cameras, of course, and I was pleased with the idea of having some really interesting Eastern chipmunk reference photos.

But my mind was already at work. The feeding station was, after all, meant for birds, not a chippie. What if? And so the finished painting tells yet another story about the funny and enchanting interactions that can occur when animals' and birds' paths cross in the wild.

Color Mixes

Use these swatches when mixing oils or matching to other paint mediums.

White + Raw Umber + Black	Burnt Sienna + Raw Sienna	Raw Sienna + White	French Ultramarine Blue + Sap Green + White	White + French Ultramarine Blue + Sap Green
Black + Sap Green	Black + Raw Umber	White + Black + Raw Umber	Black + Raw Umber + White	Burnt Sienna + White
Burnt Sienna + Raw Umber	Black + French Ultramarine Blue	Sap Green + Raw Sienna + White	White + Sap Green + Raw Sienna	Cadmium Yellow Pale + White

Line Drawing

Transfer this design to the prepared background using dark graphite paper. Be very accurate when transferring the eyes and face detail of the chipmunk, as well as the eye and beak and feather detail of the bird. When transferring the straight lines of the feeder, use a straightedge to keep them accurate. You can round and soften later as you paint.

This pattern may be hand-traced or photocopied for personal use only. Enlarge at 147% to bring it up to full size.

Materials & Reference Photos

To paint the background, you'll need:

- Hardboard (Masonite) panel, 14" x 11" x ⅛"
  (36cm x 28cm x 3mm)
- Sponge roller
- Acrylic paints by Delta Ceramcoat
  Cadet Grey
  Cactus Green
  Rainforest Green
  English Yew Green
  Hammered Iron
- Paper towels
- Protected work surface
- 320-grit wet/dry sandpaper
- Krylon Matte Finish no. 1311
- Disposable palette for oils
- Palette knife
- Odorless thinner
- Cobalt drier (optional)
- Oil paints
  Ivory Black
  Raw Umber
  Sap Green
- Cheesecloth

To paint the Chipmunk and Chickadee, you'll need:

- Oil paints
  Ivory Black
  Titanium White
  Raw Sienna
  Raw Umber
  Burnt Sienna
  Sap Green
  Cadmium Yellow Pale
  French Ultramarine
- Brushes
  nos. 0, 2, 4, 6 and 8 red sable short brights
  no. 0 red sable liner
- Odorless thinner
- Cobalt drier (optional)
- Palette knife
- Paper towels
- Disposable palette for oils
- Dark graphite paper
- Tracing paper
- Ballpoint pen
- Stylus
- Cheesecloth

Here's Ruthie's feeder, with the visiting chipmunk. Check out that culprit, stuffing those cheek pouches as fast as he can. Doesn't this photo reference just beg for a bird to come flying in?

PHOTO BY DEBORAH A. GALLOWAY

Sometimes a photo may be in the files for years before its moment arrives. That was certainly the case with this one, given to me by my friend, noted bird photographer, Arthur Morris. When I decided that a bird hanging on the side of the feeder, peeking in, would be the perfect foil for the chipmunk, this slide became the only one of our hundreds of chickadee photos that did the trick. Moral to this story: a designer can never have too many references.

PHOTO BY ARTHUR MORRIS

Background & Chickadee

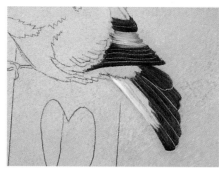

1 Review chapter 2, Painting Backgrounds, before beginning. Basecoat the Masonite panel with Cadet Grey on the top half and Rainforest Green on the bottom half, using a sponge roller. Blend between the colors with the roller as you apply them. Let dry and then sand well. For the final coat, roll Cadet Grey, Cactus Green and Rainforest Green onto the surface according to the diagram, blending between values as you apply them. Then shade the bottom left side of the surface with English Yew Green, rolling to blend into the lighter values of green. Shade the upper right side with the darker gray value of Hammered Iron, rolling to soften into the basecoat. Let dry and then sand. Spray with a matte finishing spray. Let dry overnight before transferring the design.

2 Using a no. 2 bright, base the dark feather areas on the chickadee's tail and wing with Black + Raw Umber. Draw the feather lines back into the wet paint using the stylus. Base the light values with White + Black + Raw Umber. Be very accurate, loading the brush sparingly with small amounts of paint.

3 Using the chisel edge, blend between the light and dark values on the tail. Then place very fine light feather lines with dirty white on top of each stylus line on the tail and on the wing feathers. Reload the brush with fresh, dry dirty white for *each* line. Pull the chisel edge line from the tip of the feather toward the base. Hold the brush at a 45° angle.

4 Base the bird's breast with White + Black + Raw Umber.

Base the dark area of the top feather in the stack of wing feathers with Black + Raw Umber. Fill in the narrow band at the right side with White.

Base the narrow dark band of short feathers at the near wing edge with Black + Raw Umber. Base the upper half of the back to the graphite line of the neck with Black + Raw Umber + White. Base the lighter values of gray on the back with White + a little Black + a little Raw Umber.

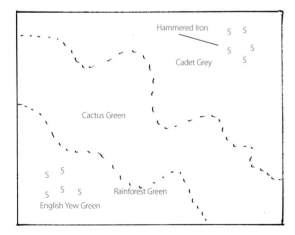

Diagram for Color Placement

S = Shading

Painting the Perfect Eye

CHIPMUNK

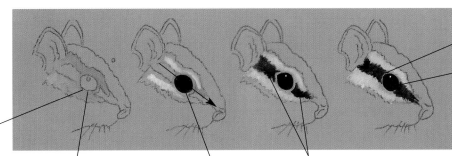

In both animals and birds, eye-rings are unfeathered or unfurred areas of skin around the eye.

This eye-ring can be filled in with the surrounding fur color.

Fill in eyes with Black. Get a clean edge and align with the beak or nose.

Add eyeline.

In this case, break the eye-ring in front using Black.

Use eyeline colors to narrow the width of the eye-ring.

Break the eye-ring in front to give more depth—to "sink" the eye.

CHICKADEE

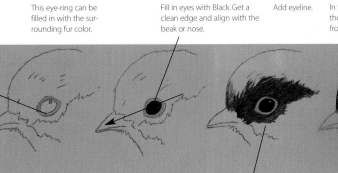

Vary the width of the eye-ring—wider at top and back, narrower at front and bottom. Then narrow the eye-ring as you work until only a hairline of eye-ring remains.

Base in the surrounding color, following the growth direction and using short strokes.

5 Blend between the values on the back of the bird. With White and a no. 2 bright, add several rows of fluffy, feathery strokes to suggest the covert feather pattern. Highlight at the top of the breast under the throat with White, and at the bottom of the belly feathers just above the tail. Chop these strokes to suggest soft, fine feathering.

Base the eye-ring with Raw Umber + a very little White on a liner. Rinse the brush in thinner and dry on a paper towel. Then fill in the eye very carefully and exactly with pure Black. Base the beak with Black + Raw Umber. Base the legs and toes with Black + Raw Umber. Use the same mix for the toe-nails.

6 Add the dot of White highlight in the eye using the liner. With a no. 0 bright, highlight the beak with a grayed white. Highlight the toes and shaft of the leg with the same mix and brush.

Base the crown, throat and nape with Black + Raw Umber, using a no. 2 bright. Where the dark mix meets the eye-ring, narrow it so it becomes just a hairline, slightly wider around the top half of the eye, and broken through to the black eye at the front corner.

7 Base the cheek with White, adding a little Raw Sienna at the right side for a warm accent. Where the white meets the dark head colors, use the chisel edge of a dry no. 2 bright to gently connect the colors, following the growth direction of the feathers. Be careful not to blend between the black and white areas. Pull tiny strokes here and there from the dark area over the gray mixes on the back to connect the head and body effectively. With a very sparse load of dirty white on a no. 2 bright, highlight the top of the head with a few feathery strokes. Using the liner, pull out a few spiky feathers under the beak.

Chipmunk

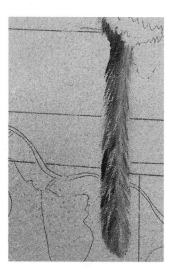

8 Base the dark values of the chipmunk's tail with Black + Raw Umber, pulling brush strokes with a no. 2 or 4 bright. Base the right side with Burnt Sienna + Raw Sienna. Allow a little background to show through under both mixes.

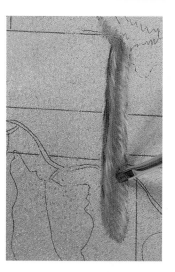

9 Come just inside the left dark edge and highlight in an uneven stripe of gray using White + Raw Umber + Black on a no. 2 bright. Highlight the right side of the tail with some strokes of a cleaner value of white, using the chisel edge of the same brush.

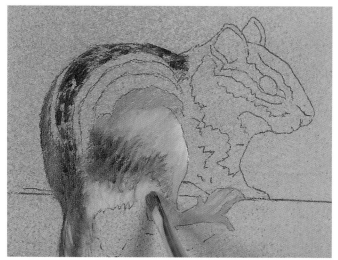

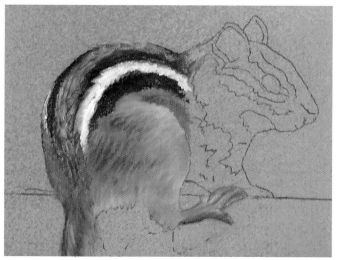

10 Base the foot with Burnt Sienna + White. Base the hip of the chipmunk on the left side with Burnt Sienna. Base a corresponding area of Burnt Sienna on the right haunch, just above the light value shown in the photo.

With Black + Raw Umber on a no. 2 bright, begin chopping in the short strokes in the ticked fur areas. One section is the wide stripe down the middle of the back, which meets the dark gray on the tail. Another area is the small section of ticking on the haunch, just above the Burnt Sienna you just applied. Remember that the denser the dark strokes, the more shadow you are creating. Compare the number of strokes you are placing to those in the photo, and add more if needed.

Finally, base the Raw Sienna and Raw Sienna + White areas of the haunch with the no. 2 bright. In all of these areas, observe the growth direction of the hair, and keep the length of your stroke compatible with the length of hair in that area.

11 With a little dirty white on the no. 2 bright, begin laying in the lighter hairs in the ticked areas. Do not use too much paint, and make eight to ten strokes before reloading the brush. Where there is more dark base, apply fewer light strokes. That helps give more depth to the shadow areas, such as at the nape of the neck. Follow growth direction as you place the light strokes.

Shade the foot with a little Raw Umber between and on the bottom of the toes. Shade the side of the chipmunk in front of the haunch with Burnt Sienna + Raw Umber. Highlight the curve of the haunch with Raw Sienna + White.

Using the no. 2 bright, place the back stripes using Black + a little Raw Umber for the dark stripes and clean white for the light stripes. The edges of the stripes should have a few short hair strokes coming out unpredictably at angles.

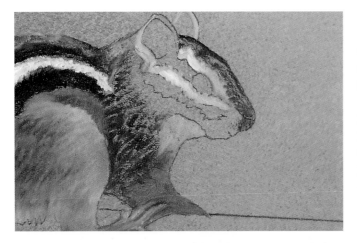

12 Base the front leg with Raw Sienna and the throat with Raw Sienna + White. Base an eyeline of Raw Sienna + White around the eye, using a no. 0 bright. Base the light facial stripes and the edges of the ears with the same mix. Base the nose with Burnt Sienna.

With a no. 0 or 2 bright, begin to chop in the very short Black + Raw Umber strokes that underlie the ticked fur on the upper front leg and side, as well as on the face between the nose and the ears. On the head, the color could almost be described as scruffy and sparse. Because the hairs are so short, it is difficult to make the basecoat for them with a chisel edge.

13 With a no. 0 bright, place the darkest value in the near ear with Black + Raw Umber. Base the lighter value in the near ear with the dirty brush + White. Base the back of the far ear with Black + Raw Umber + White, a medium-value warm gray.

Base the cheek where shown with Raw Sienna + Burnt Sienna. Highlight the nose with Burnt Sienna + White.

Rinse the no. 0 liner in odorless thinner and blot dry. Fill in the eye with pure Black.

Using the no. 0 bright, lay in the Black + Raw Umber eyeline in front and behind the eye, narrowing the eye-ring to just a fine line as the colors meet. Edges of the dark eyeline and the light facial stripes should be uneven and broken, but are too tiny to be hairy.

Now using a pale gray mix of White + Black + Raw Umber, use the no. 2 bright, and in smallest areas the no. 0 bright, to lay on the light highlights over the ticked hair areas. Use sparse paint and choppy strokes that follow the lay of the hair. Where ticked areas are adjacent to solid-color areas, walk a little of the dark and the highlight back and forth across the line where they meet to encourage the varied colors to gradate softly into one another.

14 With a no. 2 bright and White + Raw Sienna, highlight the cheek, muzzle and top of the neck. Then using Raw Umber, shade all along underneath the lower light facial stripe and down into the rusty area, as well as a bit on the muzzle.

With White on the liner, add the highlight dot in the eye. Then, with a little additional white, highlight down the middle of the widest areas of light facial stripes and the whisker pad by stippling with the liner.

When the chipmunk has dried, you can deepen and enrich the rusty areas of the fur with additional Burnt Sienna if desired. I did this on the rump above the tail and on the side of the face, as well as a bit on the haunch. Be careful to wait until the surface is dry to do these strong additions. See the finished painting on page 38 for this final accent.

Bird Feeder

15 The very darkest shadow areas on the bird feeder where the bottom of the wood shows are simply based with Black + just a tad of Raw Umber, using the flat of the no. 8 bright.

The darkest woodgrain is Black + Raw Umber also, but with more umber to warm the mix. Using the chisel edge of the larger no. 6 and no. 8 brights, lay in the dark woodgrain-like values. The intermediate areas of brownish red tones are Burnt Sienna + Raw Umber. The strongest areas of the rusty color are straight Burnt Sienna.

Create strong shadows of Black + Raw Umber under the chipmunk, the bird, and the roof line as you lay on the other dark areas. You can see in this photo how much dimension you can develop with strong darks before a speck of light is ever added. Take your time and build these necessary darks with a firm hand.

16 Fill in the top heart cutout with very dark Black + Raw Umber. Now add the light values, using Raw Umber + White, the warmest gray, and also a cooler mix of Black + Raw Umber + White. White is heavy and dense; apply these mixes sparsely so they do not take over the darks. Be patient, using small amounts of paint and extending each paint addition to the max before picking up more paint.

17 You may blend with the woodgrain between values, using the chisel edge of the no. 8 bright. You may also pat and pull some of the paint to soften, using the cheesecloth pad. The cheesecloth is particularly helpful if you got too much paint in some areas.

18 Now study the photo closely. You'll see all manner of fine and broad detailed woodgraining added on top of the blended basecoat. Paint these with an excellent no. 4 chisel edge and small amounts of thinned Black + Raw Umber. Apply very loosely, letting the brush slide along, following some natural curves as well as creating knotholes and uneven or damaged areas of the wood. Remember, this is a very weathered feeder and we don't want it to look sharp edged and overly precise.

After all graining is added, pat the areas that don't please you with the cheesecloth to soften them into the basecoat.

Morning Glories

19 Base the dark values on the morning glories with Black + French Ultramarine. Base the middle values with the same mix, adding just a smidgen of White. Base the lightest values with White on the dirty brush.

Lay in the trumpets and the flower centers with clean white, except for the very center hollow, which is left open for now. Divide the petals with White veins that are wider at flower center and narrow to a fine line at the petal's edge.

Base the dark areas of the leaves, stems and tendrils with Black + Sap Green. Base the lighter leaf values with Sap Green + Raw Sienna + White.

20 Blend between the values on the flower petals with a dry chisel, following the natural growth direction of each petal. Place stronger white highlights where needed on a few petal edges.

Shade, if desired, to strengthen the blues using straight French Ultramarine to deepen next to the centers. Fill in the central hollow of the flower centers with Raw Umber at the bottom and Cadmium Yellow Pale on the upper side of the center. Lay in the central vein with the light green leaf mix. Highlight the stems in a line down the center with the same light mix, blending slightly to round the stem to the eye. Blend the leaves with the chisel edge of no. 4 bright for smaller leaves and the no. 6 bright for larger ones. Pull strokes from the edges of the leaves toward the central vein. If the texture gets too strong, simply lower the angle of the brush to the surface to soften.

After blending, add leaf highlights using White + Sap Green + Raw Sienna.

21 Blend the white highlights on each petal. Add rolled petal edges with White in a few places to add interest. Reinforce veining in the petals if needed.

Blend the center values, pulling a little into the surrounding white to connect these areas, as though colors are coming from the trumpets and fading into the petals. Add stamens with Cadmium Yellow Pale + White.

Do the final blending of leaf highlights. On the trumpets, pull a little green from the calyxes to shade along the trumpets' sides, rounding and softening them.

22 Additional depth behind and around the left side of the feeder will make it look more tucked into the surrounding habitat. A light spray with a matte finishing spray will protect the painting as you work.

Make a mix of Black + Raw Umber + Sap Green on the palette, thinning it with a little odorless thinner and adding a drop of siccative to speed drying time. Apply this with the palette knife in thin scrapes where more color is desired.

23 Use a small pad of cheesecloth to rub and soften the colors into the background. If paint gets onto the painting itself, you can rub most off with the cheesecloth and then evaluate. Sometimes the additional glazing enhances the painting, and you may wish to leave it.

I particularly liked the dulled intensities of the bottom morning glories where a little glaze got onto them, and I decided to leave it.

But, for example, if the glaze dulls the chipmunk's white stripes, you might wish to remove it with a no. 8 bright dampened with a little odorless thinner. It will come off easily—don't worry.

Oil antiquing is a great enricher. It can work wonders for a pale or colorless piece and add tremendous depth even to a piece you were pleased with. Don't be afraid to experiment.

Opossum and Young

*O*possums hold a very special place as the only marsupial of all our North American critters, as well as one of the most primitive of our living mammals. When the minute infants are born, they find their way to the mother's fur-lined pouch and complete their development there. As teenagers, they clamber out, and Mom carries them around on her back, as you see in this painting.

About the size of a house cat, this mother is fiercely defensive of her young, and may spit and hiss to discourage predators. Active mainly at night, these interesting animals feed on a wide variety of fruits, nuts, insects and rodents, preferring suburban gardens, farmlands or woodlands near streams where they can seek shelter in hollow trees or logs. And yes, they "play possum," sometimes feigning death when cornered.

Color Mixes

Use these swatches when mixing oils or matching to other paint mediums.

Black + Raw Umber + White	Black + Raw Umber + more White	Raw Sienna + Winsor Red + White	Sap Green + Raw Sienna + White	Sap Green + Raw Sienna + more White
Raw Sienna + Winsor Red + White	Burnt Sienna + White	Raw Sienna + White	Black + Raw Umber	Burnt Sienna + Winsor Red + Raw Sienna + White
Raw Umber + Burnt Sienna + Winsor Red	Black + Sap Green	Cadmium Yellow Pale + Raw Sienna	Cadmium Yellow Pale + White	

Line Drawing

Transfer this line drawing to your prepared background using dark graphite paper. Be especially accurate when drawing the eyes, the noses and other features. Don't let fur areas "grow" outside the drawing.

This pattern may be hand-traced or photocopied for personal use only. Enlarge at 159% to bring it up to full size.

Materials & Reference Photos

To paint the background, you'll need:

- Hardboard (Masonite) panel, 14" x 11" x ⅛"
  (36cm x 28cm x 3mm)
- Sponge rollers
- Acrylic paints by Delta Ceramcoat
    Silver Pine
    Rainforest Green
    Seminole Green
    Gamal Green
- Paper towels
- Protected work surface
- 320-grit wet/dry sandpaper
- Krylon Matte Finish no. 1311

To paint the Mother Opossum and Babies, you'll need:

- Oil paints
    Ivory Black
    Titanium White
    Raw Sienna
    Raw Umber
    Burnt Sienna
    Sap Green
    Cadmium Yellow Pale
    Winsor Red
- Brushes
    nos. 0, 2, 4, 6 and 8 red sable short brights
    no. 0 red sable liner
- Odorless thinner
- Cobalt drier (optional)
- Palette knife
- Paper towels
- Disposable palette for oils
- Dark graphite paper
- Tracing paper
- Ballpoint pen
- Cheesecloth

Reference photography is invaluable, both for providing an understanding of the creature you plan to paint and for ideas about the positions and locations of the various elements you decide to include.

In these wonderful photos, what caught my eye was the way the baby hangs on the mother facing sideways, rather than straight on. Also notice how high the guard hairs fluff up over the baby's face and body. Sometimes the little one is almost hidden in her hair. And look how long her back hairs are. All this is valuable information when you're ready to paint.

PHOTOS BY TERRY R. STEELE

Reference Photos & Background

But you need more than just the animal to "tell the story" of how it lives. I wanted to suggest in this painting that the opossum is often found at garden edges, living right around us. This photo gave me the idea of including the old wood fence post, suggestive of people. The weathered gray colors also worked well with the opossum's gray and black tones.

PHOTO BY DEBORAH A. GALLOWAY

This is the pose I chose as my main reference for the finished painting. The animal appears cautious, but calm and trusting. And I like the eye contact with the viewer that seems to say, "These are *my* babies; don't even think about messing with them!"

PHOTO BY TERRY R. STEELE

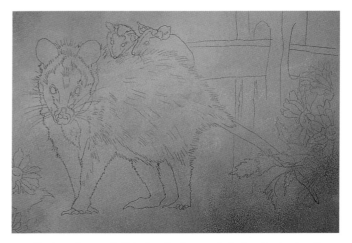

These photos of various clusters of mums provided elements to soften the edges of the painting and to balance the large form of the animal. I chose to use softer pink tones along with whites instead of the colors shown here, to connect with the pinks of the tail, noses and feet as well as the whites found in the faces of the opossums. Flowers are such lovely additions when designing a painting because they come in varied colors, allowing you to effectively manipulate them as a color unifier.

PHOTOS BY DEBORAH A. GALLOWAY

1 Review chapter 2, Painting Backgrounds, before beginning. To prepare the surface for the opossums, basecoat the Masonite panel with Silver Pine, using a sponge roller. Let dry and then sand. Re-base with a second coat of Silver Pine, and then, while the paint is still wet, drizzle a little Rainforest Green on the upper right and lower left corners of surface, using the same sponge roller to blend and soften into the background.

Now drizzle an inch or two (25mm to 51mm) of Seminole Green onto the upper left and lower right of the surface. Blend roughly into the basecoat, using a second roller. Deepen the darkest areas with a little Gamal Green and roll to blend. Finally, using the original roller, blend the edges of the darker greens so they soften into the surface. Let dry, sand and spray with Krylon Matte Finish no. 1311. Let dry overnight, and then transfer the design.

Baby Opossums

2 Load the liner with Raw Sienna +White, rolling it to a point. Outline each of the babies' eyes, creating a narrow eye-ring. Wash the brush in thinner, blot dry and tip with Black. Fill in the eyes, being careful to create a firm, smooth line between eye and eye-ring. Base the noses and each ear as shown with Burnt Sienna + White, using a small bright. Using White on the liner, add the tiny dots of highlight in the eyes. Fill in the dark areas of the ears with a no. 2 bright, using Black + Raw Umber. Wipe the brush dry, and then load in White (which becomes dirty white) and fill in the remainder of the ear as shown. Brush a bit of pinkish undercoat onto the muzzles with Burnt Sienna + White. Highlight the noses with the same mix.

3 Using Black + Raw Umber, base in the eyeline in front of and behind the eyes, narrowing the eye-rings as you come next to them.

   With the same mix, form the basecoat of the grizzled coats by chopping in underlying strokes with the chisel edge of the brush, following the natural growth direction. Bring this mix up to and into the pink edge on the muzzles and the base of the ears. Make the strokes denser and closer together in areas of shadow and more open in areas where the fur will be lighter. Omit the dark base above the eyes where light areas are more dominant.

4 Wipe the dark brush used for the basecoat strokes, and then use it to create a loading zone at edge of the white, which will become light gray. Use this mix to overlay the light fur strokes, placing color between the dark base strokes to cover the remaining background. Lay in light values above the eyes.

5 When you have finished adding the light gray, blend and soften the dark and light values with a dry brush, so the coats do not look too messy or distinct. Blend the values in the ears.

   Add cleaner white in the highlighted areas above the eyes and on the ear tips with a liner brush. Then blend with the flattened tip to give a plush, dense look. Make sure visible strokes on the head are shorter than those on the body.

   Stipple a little Burnt Sienna onto the muzzles for whisker pads, using a liner brush. Then thin a little pale gray mix and apply whiskers with a liner brush.

Mama Opossum's Face

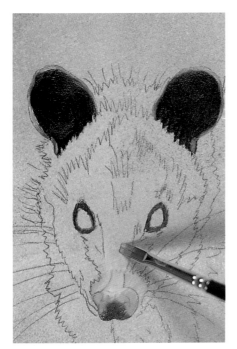

6 Fill in most of the adult's ear with Black + Raw Umber, using a no. 4 bright. Base the margin of the ear with a dirty brush + White. Lay in the eye-ring around each eye using Raw Umber and a small bright. On the nose, base the dark value with Raw Umber, the medium value with Burnt Sienna, and the lightest value with White + Raw Sienna + a bit of Winsor Red.

8 Use a bright to fill in the remaining face areas with dirty white, placing these strokes between and slightly over the dark strokes. Walk light-value edges over the dark to meld and connect. With dirty white, rough in suggestions of hair inside the ears. With a round brush, add eye highlights.

7 With a dry bright, blend the ears just a little on the line where values meet, chopping lightly with growth direction. Highlight the ear edges with a little White, stippled on with a liner.

Blend between the dark and medium values on the nose, and then highlight the top of the nosepad and down the center of the nose with White. Shade a little at the sides of the nosepad with dry Raw Umber.

Just under the curve of the eye-ring, lay a line of dirty white, using a liner brush. Then base the eye with Black.

With Black + Raw Umber, lay in choppy underlying fur strokes where shown, as well as dark eyelines in front of and behind eyes. Use brush sizes appropriate to the hair length in each area, with a no. 2 bright on the nose and around the eyes, and perhaps a no. 4 on the remainder of the head. Place darks more densely in shadow areas and less so in areas that will be highlighted. Watch growth direction carefully. When the dark areas have been applied, use a dirty brush + White for overlying areas of fur.

9 Add white highlights on the face, chopping color on first with a small bright, and then adding density and plushness with the tip of the liner loaded in very clean White.

Legs and Tail

11 Shade the bottoms of the toes with Raw Umber, using a no. 2 bright. Highlight the toes with a dirty brush + White.

Using a small bright, chop just enough dirty white fur strokes on top of the leg base-coat to indicate growth direction, roundness and volume of the hair.

10 Base the legs with Black + Raw Umber. Use a no. 4 bright, and work choppy strokes to indicate growth direction of the fur. Base nearly completely with the dark mix in areas where the fur will be very black. Base the toes with Burnt Sienna + a tad of Winsor Red + Raw Sienna + White.

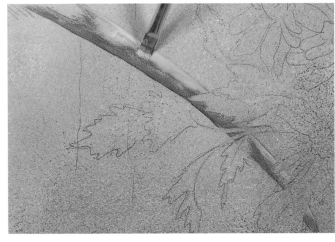

12 Base the tail, using Raw Umber + Burnt Sienna + a tad of Winsor Red for the dark value and Raw Sienna + White for the light value. Create an uneven, broken line between values.

13 Blend the tail by chopping on the line between the values to create a rough blend. When the tail has dried completely, make a mix of slightly thinned (with odorless thinner) Black + Raw Umber and apply a dark glaze to the top quarter of the tail length, as shown on the finished painting.

Body Fur and Wooden Fence

14 Using the no. 4 and no. 6 brights, begin laying in the dark-hair basecoat on the rest of the body. Remember to vary hair length and density, and follow the natural growth direction carefully. Create dense shadows next to the young opossums to give the impression that they are tucked down *in* the adult's fur.

15 Wipe the brush dry and, using a dirty brush + White, begin applying light overlay strokes, filling between the dark strokes. Notice that the hairs are quite straight at this point. Reload the brush frequently but with sparse paint. If you are too liberal with the paint, you'll get mud instead of more distinct hair-like lines. Pull a few strokes of light up over the bodies of the little ones.

16 Now you are ready to dilute the White with odorless thinner. The consistency should be very, very thin—ink-like and puddly, not holding a peak. Load the liner brush sparingly and begin to pull the fine guard hairs out from the edges of the body, as well as a few here and there in more dominant highlight areas.

Some guard hairs should be pulled up over the babies, too. Be careful not to pull hairs into the eyes. Add whiskers with the same mix. Always pull whiskers from the whisker base outward, so they can become very fine at the tips.

17 Base dark values of the fence with Black + Raw Umber, using the chisel edge of the no. 6 bright. Base the light values with a dirty brush + White. As dark values are applied, think *woodgrain*, and work the brush to create suggestions of this woodgraining from the start.

18 Blend the fence areas lightly with cheesecloth, pulling and patting with the woodgrain. This softens and de-emphasizes the graining and removes excess paint. Add detail with Raw Umber + Black, and highlights with a cleaner white than was used on the basecoat. Brush in very sparse Raw Sienna or Raw Sienna + Burnt Sienna to warm it.

Pink and White Mums

20 Set in a rough central vein on each leaf using the chisel edge and the light leaf mix. Blend between values on the leaves, with the growth direction, using the chisel edge held at a low angle to the surface. Add highlights using light leaf mix + more White. Highlight the stems down the center, using the chisel edge and light leaf mix or leaf highlight mix. Highlight and emphasize some of the grass stems with light green mixes

Blend between values on the petals, using a dry chisel. Highlight the petals with White.

Base the flower centers using Sap Green + Black for the dark value and Cadmium Yellow Pale + Raw Sienna for the light value.

19 Base dark values of the leaves with Black + Sap Green. Fill in light values with Sap Green + Raw Sienna + White.

Base the dark value of the pink and the white mums, as well as the stems, with the dark mix used for the leaves. Base the white mums' light value with white and the pink mums' light value with Raw Sienna + Winsor Red + White.

Add grass base areas with rough chisel-edge strokes of the dark leaf mix.

21 Blend highlights on the leaves with the same growth direction as before. Add final veining with leaf-highlight mix, using a good chisel, a light touch and very sparse paint. Veins should be wider at the stem end, narrowing to a hairline as they go down the leaf.

Some of the grass clusters may be softened to just a haze by rubbing with cheesecloth, as shown to the left of the bottom flower. Then fresh, detailed grasses may be painted on top. Such an approach gives more depth to the cluster of individual pieces of grass and helps the grasses meld quietly into the greens of the background.

Blend highlights on petals.

Use a liner brush to stipple between the values on the flower centers. Then stipple on Cadmium Yellow Pale + White for highlights, and soften into the center with the flattened tip of a liner brush.

Lop-Eared Rabbit and Pansies

S ome critters beg to be cuddled. With their darling, droopy ears, big eyes and fur as soft as a down pillow, lop babies steal your heart for sure. They have sweet, affectionate natures, are very fastidious animals and can even be house-trained.

The lop-eared bunny is the oldest kind of domestic rabbit, with the first lops dating back to the 1700s. They have been popular for show and as pets in Europe for many years, but were introduced into the United States only in the 1970s.

The English Lop is the oldest breed, and the Dwarf Lop is one of the most popular pets. But the Holland Lop is the smallest, weighing in at less than 4 pounds (1.3kg). And just for the record, you feline and canine fanciers, there are more rabbits shown in the United States than cats and dogs!

Color Mixes

Use these swatches when mixing oils or matching to other paint mediums.

Raw Sienna + White	Raw Sienna + Raw Umber	Burnt Sienna + White	Burnt Sienna + Purple Madder Alizarin + White	Black + Raw Umber

Black + Sap Green	Burnt Sienna + White	Burnt Sienna + White + Raw Umber	White + Raw Umber	Raw Sienna + Burnt Sienna + Cadmium Yellow Pale

Burnt Sienna + Raw Umber	Purple Madder Alizarin + White	Sap Green + Raw Sienna + White	White + Sap Green + Raw Sienna

Line Drawing

Transfer this design to the prepared background using dark
graphite paper. Be very accurate
when transferring the eye, nose
and other facial features, as well
as the detail of the pansies.

This pattern may be hand-traced
or photocopied for personal use
only. Enlarge at 120% to bring it
up to full size.

Materials & Reference Photos

To paint the background, you'll need:

- Hardboard (Masonite) panel, 12" x 9" x ⅛"
- Sponge rollers
- Acrylic paints by Delta Ceramcoat
    Moss Green
    Cadet Grey
    Sachet Pink
    Wild Rose
    English Yew Green
    Oyster White
- Acrylic retarder
- Paper towels
- Protected work surface
- 320-grit wet/dry sandpaper
- Krylon Matte Finish no. 1311
- Disposable palette for oils
- Palette knife
- Odorless thinner
- Cobalt drier (optional)
- Oil paints
    Raw Umber
    Sap Green
- Cheesecloth

To paint the Lop-eared Rabbit and Pansies, you'll need:

- Oil paints
    Ivory Black
    Titanium White
    Raw Sienna
    Raw Umber
    Burnt Sienna
    Sap Green
    Cadmium Yellow Pale
    Purple Madder Alizarin
- Brushes
    nos. 0, 2, 4, 6 and 8 red sable short brights
    no. 0 red sable liner
- Odorless thinner
- Cobalt drier (optional)
- Palette knife
- Paper towels
- Disposable palette for oils
- Dark graphite paper
- Tracing paper
- Ballpoint pen
- Cheesecloth
- Krylon Satin Varnish no. 7002

A good reference photo can make or break your painting. It's important to have as much information as you can get in the shot and that it be as sharp and in focus as possible. But sometimes getting that kind of shot is a challenge.

When Kathy Kipp, my editor and good friend, asked me to include a lop in this book, I was enthused. But we had a dearth of references for this critter. Fast forward to the pet store at the local mall—baby lops! darling, wonderful and so cute. Deb grabbed the camera and took this single picture, just before we were summarily ejected from the shop by the furious owner. Nothing we could say would change his mind—and that's why this reference photo could have been a whole lot better. Moral: *always* ask permission first.

PHOTO BY DEBORAH A. GALLOWAY

Getting the pansy reference was a whole lot less stressful. A good friend owns a nursery where we have limitless opportunities to shoot all the gorgeous blooms we need. And she's never once called out the bouncer.

One last note. Both the rabbits and the pansies were shot from a "bunny's eye" view. Your subjects need to be "on the level" with each other.

PHOTO BY DEBORAH A. GALLOWAY

Background & Rabbit's Eye

1 Review the Background Preparation instructions in chapter 2 before beginning.

Base a 14" × 11" Masonite panel with Moss Green, using a sponge roller. Let dry and then sand smooth.

Rebase with the same color, adding a drizzle of retarder to keep the surface workable while adding the other colors. In the upper right corner, drizzle a little Cadet Grey and use the roller to soften it into the background Then move a little to other areas. In the central area of the surface, drizzle a little Sachet Pink and a little Wild Rose, and repeat the process, blending to soften the colors into the background and moving the colors into other areas to balance. Now on the scrap paper covering your work surface, run a sponge roller into a drizzle of Oyster White. Use this color to highlight around the pinks in the center area of the surface.

Finally, around the edges of the surface, shade a bit with a drizzle or two of English Yew Green, using a clean roller to blend into the background.

Let dry overnight and then sand smooth. Spray with Krylon Matte Finish no. 1311. When using retarder, allow extra drying time before sanding and spraying.

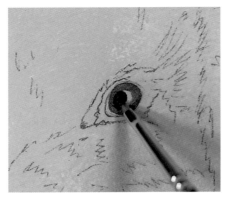

2 Base the iris with Raw Umber, using a no. 0 liner. Around the ends of the iris in the corners of the eye, place a small area of Burnt Sienna + White. Rinse the brush in thinner, blot dry and load in clean Black. Base the pupil carefully.

4 On top of the lightest lowlight value in the pupil, place a dot of clean White, using the liner brush.

Lay a fine line of Black around and just inside the iris edge, using the liner brush. Blend the inner edge of this line slightly into the Raw Umber iris using the point of the liner.

Using the no. 0 bright, outline the eye-ring around the eye with a little Raw Umber. Then shade in front of and behind the eye with the same color. Highlight the skin area around the eye with a little White + Raw Umber.

Base the fur area that comes up to the eye-ring with Raw Sienna + White.

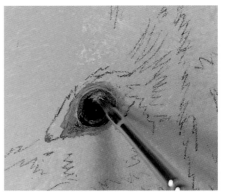

3 Dry the brush and use the corner to blend the very edges of the pupil into the Raw Umber iris.

Now lay a narrow band of Burnt Sienna + Raw Umber + White entirely around the eye. Lay the pupil lowlight using White + Raw Umber. Blend the edges into the pupil. Do not overwork.

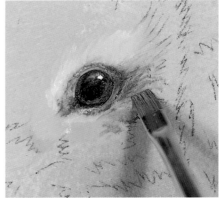

5 With the no. 2 bright, add additional shading behind the eye on top of the pale fur basecoat with Raw Umber. Blend just a little. Highlight the fur above the eye with White. Then with the corner of the chisel, connect the fur edge into the eye-ring edge to soften the line where they meet.

Face

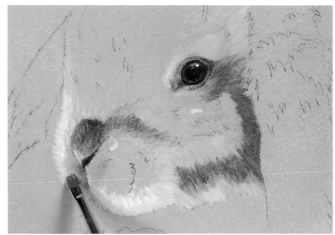

6 Using a no. 2 bright, base the darkest nose value with Raw Umber and the lighter areas with Raw Sienna + Raw Umber. Add the nostril with Black. Place a shadow under the nose with Burnt Sienna + White.

Begin applying shadows on the face from the nose around the cheek, using Raw Umber + Raw Sienna and a no. 4 bright. Extend this shadow up under the eye until it meets the dark shading previously placed behind and under the eye.

Vary stroke length with hair length in each of the areas of the face and body.

7 Highlight the bottom of the nose with White, blending in tiny choppy strokes with the no. 0 bright.

Lay on Raw Sienna below the nose at the whisker pad edges. Then add pale Raw Sienna + White where shown: around the bottoms of the whisker pads, and next to and around the umber areas above the nose and on the cheek.

8 Base the remainder of the head with Raw Sienna + Burnt Sienna + a tiny amount of Cadmium Yellow Pale using the no. 4 bright. Chop the colors on with the chisel of the brush, following the lie of the hair carefully, and making sure the stroke length is compatible with the hair length in each area.

9 Blend between value areas with the chisel edge of the brush, walking strokes back and forth across the line where values meet. Add shading with Burnt Sienna + Raw Umber, and, in the deepest areas, with just Raw Umber.

Add highlights with Raw Sienna + White, chopping light values on in the same manner as you did the basecoat. Then, add a little pinkish accent by the mouth below the nose with Purple Madder Alizarin + White.

Lop Ears

11 Before blending the ears, note the growth direction: hairs do not necessarily conform to the lengthwise line of the ear, but rather come off to the side at an angle in several places, and straight back toward the back at the top of the ear. Using the chisel, blend between the values, using the chisel to create brush marks that indicate the correct lie and length of the rabbit's hair.

Then apply any additional shading needed with Raw Umber, and highlight down the center line of the near ear and at edge of the far ear using Raw Sienna + White.

10 Finish blending, working the brush between values to connect them. To help achieve contour and form, be sure the lay of the hair is correct.

Add whisker marks with Raw Umber on the liner brush. Break up the edges of the head, pulling out fine strokes of the color in each area. Add soft, strong lights on the chin, cheek and top of the head with White on the round brush.

Using a no. 4 bright, base the ears, using Raw Umber for the darkest value and Burnt Sienna + Purple Madder Alizarin + White (adding a tad of Raw Sienna to dull the mix a bit) for the pinkish mid value. Fill in the palest areas with Raw Sienna + White

Use Raw Sienna + Burnt Sienna + a bit of Cadmium Yellow Pale above the ear in the mid-value warm area, a little Raw Umber to the left of it for a darker value and Raw Sienna + White for the lightest value, on top of the head.

12 Blend the shading and highlighting on the ears. The rest of the chest and body is based in three values: Dark—Raw Umber, Medium—Raw Sienna + Burnt Sienna + a tad of Cadmium Yellow Pale, Light—Raw Sienna + White.

Note once again that brush strokes, as you apply color, should follow the lie of the hair and reflect the hair length. Some areas you'll want to use the no. 4, others the no. 6.

Fur

13 Using the brushes with which you applied the basecoats, begin blending on the line where the values meet. It is as important to achieve good gradations between values as it is to have those values. Insufficient blending will make your bunny look spotty rather than contoured.

Fluff out lighter values using a no. 4 bright with White + Raw Sienna. Let some of these hairs soften the body edges as they did on the face. Guard hairs give a fluffy feeling to the fur, but must not be overdone.

Using the no. 4 bright, add additional shading on the back next to the ear, using Raw Umber.

14 Blend the shading on the back. Next, add additional Raw Umber + Raw Sienna for more depth on the chest where the rabbit's body is behind the pansies and leaves, where the ear folds over the head, and around the eye. Then, shade with Raw Umber above the nose.

Thin a little White and apply long whiskers with the round brush. Don't pull whisker lines over the pansies; remember, they're in front of the rabbit.

15 Blend the shading applied in the previous step with the growth direction, using the no. 4 bright.

Give the eye its final shape, using the liner and a bit of Black + Raw Umber to break the eye-ring in front of the eye into the tear area. Add additional Raw Umber shading if needed to make sure the eye is seated well within the fur around it.

Pansies

16 Basecoat the pansy petals with Raw Sienna + White, using the no. 2 or no. 4 bright. Base the dark values on the leaves and the stems with Black + Sap Green.

17 Highlight overlapping edges, the tops of rolls, as well as some petal edges with White. Use a no. 2 bright and apply sparse paint with pressure. Do not continue white all around the edge of a petal; apply light hits in areas, but not in outlines.

Fill in remaining areas of leaves with the light value of Sap Green + Raw Sienna + White. Highlight the stems with the same mix, pulling a line down the center of each stem, then blending on the edges of it just a bit to create a little value gradation between the light value and the dark basecoat.

18 Blend the white pansy highlights in the growth direction, using the chisel edge for natural texture.

Base the pansy face with Purple Madder Alizarin.

Using the light green leaf mix, lay a rough central vein in each leaf as a blending guide. Now blend the leaves from edge to center vein at the lateral vein angle, using the chisel edge of a dry no. 2 or no. 4 bright. If leaves appear too textured, lower the brush angle.

Place leaf highlights with White + Sap Green + Raw Sienna, using the no. 4 bright.

19 With a very dry no. 2 bright, cut the corner of the chisel into the edge of the face color. Do not blend the colors together with the flat of the brush, but rather use the chisel to skizzle back and forth just on the line where the colors meet. Here and there, pull a chisel line or two out from the dark to give definition to the petal.

Then, using the same brush, which will have a little dirty Purple Madder Alizarin on it, shade a bit on the back petals to help them recede. Blending should follow the growth direction of each petal.

Blend the leaf highlights. Add a little Purple Madder Alizarin accent color, if desired. Blend with a chisel stroke, just as you did in the other steps. Add final vein structure with the light value mix.

20 The white that surrounds the pansy center is actually the petal edge, which rolls over so that you can see the other side. Apply these fuzzy areas of white with the liner.

At the top of the upside down V, add a tiny triangle of Sap Green + Black. Below that, add a small scallop of Cadmium Yellow Pale. Then, with the round brush, blend just a bit between the green and yellow areas.

The edges of the yellow and the white should be fuzzy and broken where they fall over the petals.

Antiquing Glaze

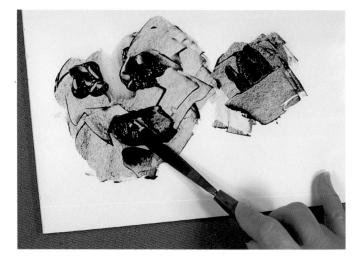

21 Normally, I do my antiquing directly on the dry surface, without spraying first. But if the oil paint is still "tender" (uncured) and I were to decide to remove the glaze for some reason, the thinner might well remove very small amounts of paint.

If you've never done this kind of glazing before, you may wish to spray the finished painting lightly with Krylon Matte Finish no. 1311 prior to antiquing. Then the painting is totally safe, even if you put on and take off the glaze several times.

Two mixes are used for antiquing on the finished painting. On the right is a slightly thinned patty of Raw Umber, and on the left you see I'm making a mix that is half Sap Green and half Raw Umber, also slightly thinned. A drop of drier may be added to each to speed drying time.

22 Using the palette knife, I scrape thin swatches of each mix here and there on the surface where I want to increase the depth or simply add more interest.

23 Use a soft pad of cheesecloth to blend the edges of each scrape of paint, leaving some areas darker and removing more paint in other areas for lighter values. It's perfectly acceptable if some of the glazing gets into the design area; I simply buff it off with the cheesecloth. Or if I like the effect, I let it be.

24 As I was completing the glazing of this piece, I wished the pansies had turned out a bit warmer. So I took a bit of Raw Sienna on a no. 4 bright and scruffed a bit over the shadow areas in the back petals and where the front pansy overlaps the back one. I then buffed off the excess Raw Sienna. Look at the photo of the finished painting; you can see how the warmer tones in the foreground flowers make the overall look of the painting much softer.

When all glazing is dry, the painting may be sprayed with a final finish of Krylon Satin Varnish no. 7002.

Eastern Gray Squirrel and Queen Butterfly

The Eastern Gray belongs to the larger family of tree squirrels—an appropriate name since they are closely tied to their arboreal lifestyle. Hardwood forests, replete with the favored nuts, seeds, fungi and fruits that provide most of the food for this animal, are the main habitat.

Tree squirrels have the well-known habit of burying seeds and nuts for future use—and then forgetting about at least some of them, giving rise to new growth. In fact, tree squirrels are one of the most important reforestation agents in their range.

Even so, folks with a penchant for feeding birds sometimes rue the day when this tenacious and wily animal finds their feeders. More often than not, the squirrel scores high against the many "squirrel-proof" feeders, and it's evident when you see those bulging cheeks filled with your best sunflower seed.

Color Mixes

Use these swatches when mixing oils or matching to other paint mediums.

Raw Sienna + Raw Umber

Black + Raw Umber

White + Black + Raw Umber

Black + Sap Green

Sap Green + Raw Sienna + White

White + Sap Green + Raw Sienna

White + Raw Umber

Raw Sienna + White

Burnt Sienna + White

Burnt Sienna + Raw Sienna + White

Alizarin Crimson + Winsor Red + Raw Sienna

Raw Sienna + White

Alizarin Crimson + Winsor Red + Burnt Sienna

Alizarin Crimson + Winsor Red + Burnt Sienna + White

~ Sherry C. Nelson ~

Line Drawing

Transfer this design to the prepared back-ground with dark graphite paper. Be accurate and painstaking as you do the details of the head, the eye and the intricate patterning of the butterfly. Take care with the flower detail too. Remember, the better the transfer, the better the painting.

This pattern may be hand-traced or photocopied for personal use only. Enlarge at 133% to bring it up to full size.

Materials & Reference Photos

To paint the background, you'll need:

- Hardboard (Masonite) panel, 14" x 11" x ⅛"
  (36cm x 28cm x 3mm)
- Sponge roller
- Acrylic paints by Delta Ceramcoat
  - Seminole Green
  - Gamal Green
  - Leaf Green
  - Village Green
- Paper towels
- Protected work surface
- 320-grit wet/dry sandpaper
- Krylon Matte Finish no. 1311

To paint the Eastern Gray Squirrel and Queen Butterfly, you'll need:

- Oil paints
  - Ivory Black
  - Titanium White
  - Raw Sienna
  - Raw Umber
  - Burnt Sienna
  - Sap Green
  - Cadmium Yellow Pale
  - Winsor Red
  - Alizarin Crimson
- Brushes
  - nos. 0, 2, 4, 6 and 8 red sable short brights
  - no. 0 red sable liner
- Odorless thinner
- Cobalt siccative (optional)
- Palette knife
- Paper towels
- Disposable palette for oils
- Dark graphite paper
- Tracing paper
- Ballpoint pen
- Cheesecloth

Here's the typical squirrel pose: chowing down on some yummy nut or seed stolen from your feeder. To me, this animal seems ordinary, and there's no point in consigning it to a piece of artwork.

That's something to consider when photographing your backyard critters. Set up situations that yield unusual and unique photos, ones that justify the time and effort you spend in the creation of a new painting.

PHOTO BY TERRY R. STEELE

Here's the alternative I chose. This animal appears much more in touch with its surroundings and interactive with the world around it. To me, this kind of photo has a lot of potential as a reference shot—as a starting point to tell a story of some kind about the squirrel's world from the squirrel's point of view. What is it looking at? What is it thinking about doing? The answers make a painting more exciting.

PHOTO BY TERRY R. STEELE

Reference Photos & Background

The choice of flower came easily. Wild roses are typical of many woodland areas, and I wanted the complementary color to play against the strong greens of the deep forest setting.

This shot is especially helpful because it shows full-blown flowers, partially open ones, as well as buds and leaves. There's lots of information here to help you when you sit down to apply paint to a surface.

PHOTO BY TERRY R. STEELE

Butterflies are lovely creatures to include in any painting, but especially so in one that needs a bit of action to balance a more static focal area. The busy, active feeding mode of the Queen butterfly is a perfect foil for the quietness of the observant squirrel.

PHOTO BY DEBORAH A. GALLOWAY

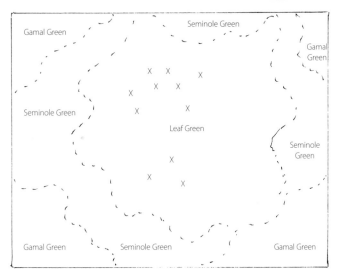

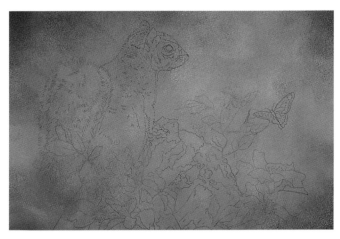

Diagram for Color Placement

X = Village Green

1 Review chapter 2, Painting Backgrounds, before beginning. Basecoat the Masonite panel with Seminole Green. Let dry and then sand until the surface is smooth. Re-base with three different values of green—Gamal Green, Seminole Green and Leaf Green—placed as shown on the diagram. Blend between them to achieve a splotchy, irregular, out-of-focus look for the background. Drizzle a little Village Green onto the upper central area of the surface, and blend a little to highlight and to control the intensity of the stronger greens. Let dry, and the be sure to sand well and spray with Krylon Matte Finish no. 1311.

Squirrel's Face

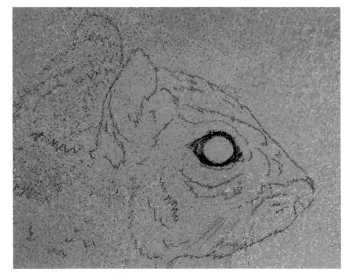

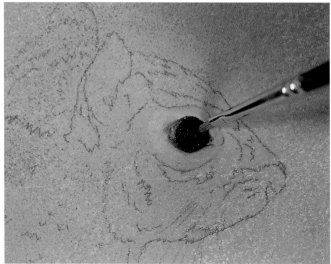

2 Lay the Raw Umber eye-ring around the outside of the squirrel's eye, using a no. 0 bright. In the front and back corners of the eye, highlight on top of the eye-ring with a little Raw Umber + White.

3 Rinse out the brush in thinner, blot it dry on a paper towel and load with clean Black. Base the eye pupil neatly and carefully. With a no. 2 bright, lay Raw Sienna + White just outside of the eye-ring in a wide band around the eye.

4 With a little grayed White, lay the lowlight in the eye. With a dry brush, blend the lowlight just at the edges of the color, not all over the eye. The color should remain quite localized, but the value should gradate into the black base.

Highlight with a very light value of White + Raw Sienna above and below the eye on the Raw Sienna basecoat. Don't let the white continue around to the corners of the eye.

5 With the liner brush, add the final highlight dot in the eye. Blend the highlight on the eye-ring with the no. 0 liner, stippling to get a dense look to the very short fur in that area. Shade the eye-ring in front and in back of the eye with Raw Sienna.

Begin placing dark shadow values on the face and near the ear with Raw Umber, using the no. 2 bright. Use short chops of the chisel edge of the brush and establish the growth direction of the hair even at this early point.

Face & Head

6 Base around the dark values of the face and ears with Raw Sienna. Use Raw Sienna + White to base down onto the throat and chin, as well as on the muzzle beneath the nose.

7 With a dry brush, begin connecting the dark- and lighter-value areas of fur color, chopping on the line where the colors meet the chisel edge. Work in the growth direction, and leave some texture to tell the story of the fur in each area. Do not overwork; colors can become muddy.

Blend carefully between the light-value band around the eye and the dark-value surrounding it. Pull light values slightly into the dark, and vice versa so that the light band connects realistically to the colors around it.

Highlight with Burnt Sienna + White on the nose. Highlight with White + Raw Sienna on the cheek and chin of the squirrel.

8 With clean White and a clean no. 0 bright, lay the very white tufts of fur behind the ears. This dramatic feature is a field mark of the Eastern Gray Squirrel and thus is very important to the realism of the painting.

The remaining fur on the squirrel's head is agouti, or ticked. Lay the Black + Raw Umber basecoat on in these areas with a small bright and short strokes so that the fur direction is established and hair length correctly suggested.

Add whiskers with a liner and very thin Black paint.

9 Pick up White + Raw Umber + Black on the no. 2 bright and begin laying the pale gray surface hair to the ticked areas. Use the same short brush strokes and follow the lay of the hair so that the salt-and-pepper look to the hair is correctly established.

Body & Legs

10 The squirrel's body has underlying warm tones in some areas of the ticked hair. Base with Raw Sienna first in the areas shown, and then begin laying the dark values of Black + Raw Umber on top in short strokes, following the growth direction of the squirrel's hair.

11 Complete the darks which underlie the ticked fur. Remember to make dark strokes denser and closer together in areas which will be more shaded, and a bit farther apart and looser in areas which will have the lightest values. Notice also how the hair direction flares out and over the hip of the squirrel. Those direction changes are very important to create the form and dimension of the body.

Base the toes on the front foot with Burnt Sienna + Raw Sienna + White.

12 Shade between the toes with a bit of Raw Umber on the no. 0 bright. Highlight on the tops of the toes with White + Burnt Sienna.

Use additional dark mix to shade in the strongest shadow areas, which include the back and bottom of the squirrel and under the tail and where the leg is next to the body. Do this before applying any light values.

Using the no. 2 in areas of shorter fur and the no. 4 in areas of longer, begin applying the White + Raw Umber light-value strokes to complete the ticked fur areas. The brush should be dry and loaded sparsely, and you should make eight or ten strokes before reloading. The same mix can be carefully based along the edge of the haunch and the edge of the front.

13 Fluff and pull fine hairs out from the areas of light at the body's edge with the liner brush as shown. Make them very fine and almost perpendicular to the line of the animal's body.

Base the toenails with the black mix.

Squirrel's Tail

14 Base the tail at the top with underlying Raw Sienna accent color. Then begin laying in the Black + Raw Umber base for the ticking, this time with larger brushes and, consequently, longer hair strokes. A no. 4 bright would be good to start with, and some of the longest hairs at the bottom of the tail could well be done with the no. 6 bright.

Notice that the hair pattern is almost a sunburst from the center of the tail top, with the most dense dark in that area, and that the bottommost hairs are a little squiggly, not quite as straight as the shorter hairs in other areas of the body.

Leave areas for light values open until all darks are applied. Study the perspective before beginning to apply the White. In this view, you see the edge of the tail as it extends from the body and then rolls over toward the viewer.

15 Add initial light values of white in the ticked fur areas with the same brights you used to apply the basecoat colors. Brushstroke length should be similar, and growth direction as well. Use short choppy strokes and a sparsely-loaded brush.

With a clean no. 2 bright, apply a sparse, narrow and irregular dirty white base along edge of the tail. Use the chisel to blend the edge unevenly into the ticked hairs. Then, with thinned White paint on the liner brush, pull guard hairs over the white base as well as over the junction where the light edge meets darker areas of colors.

When the tail is dry, lay subtle black shading next to the white edge, using a no. 2 bright. This bit of color is quite dramatic and makes the tail look more realistic. See the finished painting on pages 70-71 for this addition.

Tree Stump & Wild Roses

16 The old stump on which the squirrel sits is based with Raw Umber in the darkest areas, particularly next to and under the squirrel, as well as under the foliage. Use Raw Sienna in middle-value areas, and White + Raw Umber in the lighter areas at the outer tip of the log. Be sure to go carefully around the roses and leaves to retain the pattern. Blend colors with the length of the stump, using the chisel edge.

17 Apply Black + Raw Umber detail with the brights first, laying in major areas of woodgrain. Emphasize shadows as well with a blacker value of the same mix.

On top of the first graining, you may now apply Black + Raw Umber detail linework with the liner brush, as well as thinned White between the dark veins, also stippled on with the liner.

If any areas appear too busy or if the paint is too heavy, soften the look by patting a bit with a pad of cheesecloth.

18 Basecoat all the dark values on the leaves and the stems with Black + Sap Green. Keep the edges of the darks ragged so they will blend easily with the lighter values.

Basecoat the darker values on the petals with Alizarin Crimson + Winsor Red + Raw Sienna, again letting the edge of the value be broken and uneven. Fill in the lighter values with Raw Sienna + White, which should be applied with sparse paint on the brush.

19 Blend between values on the petals, using a dry chisel edge. Add the clean White at the base of each petal. Base the round flower center with Sap Green + Black + a little White.

Make a mix of Sap Green + Raw Sienna + White and base the remaining areas of all the leaves.

20 Lay in a light-value green central vein in each leaf. Use the chisel edge of the no. 2 or no. 4 bright and pull from the leaf edge at an angle toward the central vein line. Blend each leaf. If the lines appear too harsh, simply lower the angle of the brush to the surface while blending.

Use the light green mix to highlight down the center line of each stem. Blend highlights slightly at the edges to round the stem to the eye.

Make a lighter-value green mix of White + Sap Green + Raw Sienna and add a few highlights on some leaf edges. Reblend in the same growth direction.

Blend just a little where the white value of the flower centers joins the pink petals.

Use slightly thinned Cadmium Yellow Pale applied with the liner brush for the stamens and the pollen dots.

21 Using a little pale green, stipple highlights on the rose centers with the liner brush.

Add additional lights and rolled edges on the rose petals with more White. Blend the edges of the highlights to soften.

Queen Butterfly

22 Base the reddish areas of the butterfly's wings with Alizarin Crimson + Winsor Red + Burnt Sienna, using the no. 2 bright. Then, highlight at the edges of the reddish mix, underneath where the white spots will fall, using a little of the same mix + White. Blend into the wing to a soft gradation.

Using the no. 0 bright, base in the dark borders around the wings using Black + just a little Raw Umber. Use the corner of the chisel to edge the black here and there into the margins of the red to disrupt the border so it appears natural. Then, base the body with the same dark mix.

23 Thin the dark mix with a little odorless thinner, and apply fine section lines and antennae with the liner brush.

Add tiny white dots with same brush, using White. Vary dot size a little; the larger ones appear on the forewings at the point and gradually get smaller as they go down the wing.

24 When the painting is dry, dull the more intense flowers by applying a little glaze of Sap Green + Alizarin Crimson. Choose those blossoms least focal and scruff a little of this mix onto some of the petals with a sparsely-loaded brush.

Then choose the most focal petals and add white highlights with a small clean bright.

Blend the highlights with a dry brush. If they don't blend smoothly, rub the edge of the highlight with the cheesecloth a bit to soften.

Wipe off any excess green glaze and blend into the petals with a small pad of cheesecloth.

Don't be afraid to tackle these steps at the end of a painting. On a dry surface, anything you add can easily be removed with a little odorless thinner.

Whitetail Fawn & Chipmunk

We were driving a group of painting students up a mountainous road to the high country for birding early one morning. Coming around a curve, we saw a lovely doe, standing just off the gravel road in the grasses. We stopped; she stared. Cameras snapped. But still, she didn't leave. Suddenly, the reason presented itself. A newborn fawn began stirring under her feet, struggling to take those first steps. Finally, after a bit of a bumble, it stood on spindly legs and had its first breakfast. Then, ever so slowly, the doe led the fawn into the trees and out of sight.

Not one of us who was there that day has ever forgotten the thrill. Wildlife watching is infinitely rewarding, and every single trip yields some new insight that enriches one's life. Buy a pair of binoculars, borrow a field guide, pack a lunch and get out there!

Color Mixes

Use these swatches when mixing oils or matching to other paint mediums.

Burnt Sienna + White	Burnt Umber + Raw Umber	Burnt Sienna + Burnt Umber + Raw Umber	Burnt Umber + Black	Burnt Umber + Burnt Sienna + Raw Sienna
White + Raw Umber	Black + Sap Green	Sap Green + Raw Sienna + White	Raw Sienna + White	Black + Raw Umber + Burnt Umber
Burnt Sienna + Raw Sienna	Burnt Sienna + Burnt Umber	Black + Raw Umber	Raw Umber + White	White + Sap Green + Raw Sienna
Alizarin Crimson + Winsor Violet + Raw Sienna	Cadmium Yellow Pale + White			

Line Drawing

Transfer this design to
the prepared back-
ground using dark
graphite paper. Be very
accurate, as always,
when transferring eyes
and facial features on
both animals. Keep the
fur within the pattern
lines—don't let it
"grow" beyond the
design.

This pattern may be
hand-traced or photo-
copied for personal use
only. Enlarge at 161% to
bring it up to full size.

Materials & Reference Photos

To paint the background, you'll need:

- Hardboard (Masonite) panel, 14" x 11" x ⅛"
  (36cm x 28cm x 3mm)
- Sponge roller
- Acrylic paints by Delta Ceramcoat
    Silver Pine
    Cactus Green
    Rainforest Green
- Paper towels
- Protected work surface
- 320-grit wet/dry sandpaper
- Krylon Matte Finish no. 1311

To paint the Whitetail Fawn and Chipmunk, you'll need:

- Oil Paints
    Ivory Black
    Titanium White
    Raw Sienna
    Raw Umber
    Burnt Sienna
    Burnt Umber
    Sap Green
    Cadmium Yellow Pale
    Alizarin Crimson
    Winsor Violet
- Brushes
    nos. 0, 2, 4, 6 and 8 red sable short brights
    no. 0 red sable liner
- Odorless thinner
- Cobalt drier (optional)
- Palette knife
- Paper towels
- Disposable palette for oils
- Dark graphite paper
- Tracing paper
- Ballpoint pen
- Cheesecloth
- Stylus

Sometimes good fortune smiles on you, and I'm sure my friend Terry Steele felt that way the morning he happened on this whitetail fawn.

If you ever discover a fawn like this, lying still as a mouse, you may rest assured that the mother has not abandoned it. She is nearby, and the best thing you can do is to let it be and let the mother return to her infant. Don't be tempted to touch the little one, and don't even walk near it; your trail could lead a predator to the baby.

PHOTO BY TERRY R. STEELE

Some color was needed to enhance the fawn painting, but I didn't want large flower forms that would distract from the interaction between the stars of this show. The phlox seemed a perfect solution, and when combined with grasses, they are just about the right height to allow us a look into the life of this newborn.

PHOTO BY TERRY R. STEELE

Reference Photos & Background

Cliff Chipmunks are common members of the larger ground squirrel family, and different species are found throughout most of North America. They are nosy and inquisitive—and I have no trouble believing that the one in the painting was just as astonished to discover the newborn fawn as the fawn was to suddenly be eye-to-eye with one of its neighbors. Talk about a story to tell!

A good way to photograph small animals and birds is to set up a water drip. This can be as simple as a gallon plastic container of water with a tiny hole punched in the bottom and hung on a tree limb over a shallow clay saucer. In the desert, water is more of a magnet than food, and at a remote campsite you'll soon find yourself surrounded by wildlife.

PHOTOS BY DEBORAH A. GALLOWAY

1 Review chapter 2, Painting Backgrounds, before beginning.
Basecoat the Masonite panel with Silver Pine, using a sponge roller. Let dry and then sand smooth. Rebase with the same color, and then drizzle some Cactus Green on the top half of the surface and some Rainforest Green on the bottom half. Using the same roller, blend and soften these colors into the background, moving some here and some there to balance them across the surface. Allow the panel to dry and then sand again. Spray lightly with Krylon Matte Finish no. 1311. Wait overnight before transferring the design.

Painting the Realistic Eye

THE REALISTIC EYE

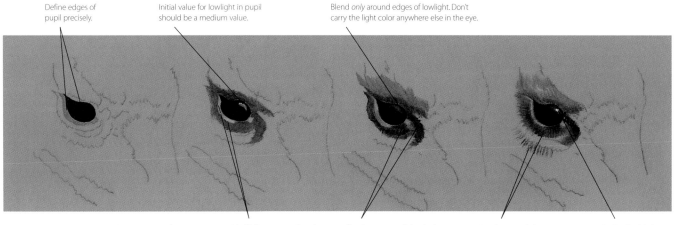

Define edges of pupil precisely.

Initial value for lowlight in pupil should be a medium value.

Blend *only* around edges of lowlight. Don't carry the light color anywhere else in the eye.

Use paint sparsely but firmly.

Highlights are not placed continuously—breaking them gives natural value changes.

Shading on top of the shadow surrounding the eye helps "sink" it—gives it more depth.

Note the growth direction as surrounding dark is connected to light-value skin around the eye.

The final highlight is placed on top of the lightest value of lowlight.

2 Use a no. 2 bright for the following steps.
Base the eye-ring with Burnt Sienna + Raw Sienna + White. Lay dark shading around the eye-ring with Burnt Umber + Raw Umber.

Lay in the mouth line and the narrow edge around the nosepad with Burnt Sienna + White. Place Raw Sienna + White around the mouth and on the lips.

Base the nosepad with Black. Base the dark value on top of the nose with Black + Raw Umber + Burnt Umber. Base the light value with White. The dark above the nose and on the muzzle is Black + Raw Umber + Burnt Umber, applied with a no. 4 bright.

3 Blend at the mouth line to make it less distinct.
Blend between values on top of the nosepad. Blend the dark of the muzzle slightly into the light lip area to break the hard line between those color areas. Highlight the nosepad with a dirty brush + White, blending to soften the color. Then rehighlight with a stronger catchlight of pure White.

With a clean no. 0 bright, base the entire eye with Black. Apply the lowlight, blend slightly and then add a stronger White highlight dot.

With the liner brush, add Raw Sienna stippling on the whisker pads.

4 Base the rest of the head, neck and ears using a no. 4 bright. As you apply color, think ahead about the lay of the hair and direction of growth, and chop the colors onto the surface with the brush chisel held parallel to that direction. Establishing the movement of the hair on the head and body early on will give you better dimension in your animal later.

The darkest values are Burnt Umber + Raw Umber, which are found at the base of the ears, and in the shadow areas on the top of the head and between the legs.

A medium value of Burnt Sienna + Raw Sienna is placed on the ears, on top of the head and in rusty patches in front of and behind the eye.

The lower light value of Raw Sienna and the lighter value of Raw Sienna + White are placed in the remaining areas of the ears, chin and throat.

5 Now begin blending between the values you just placed, again following growth direction, and using the same brushes you did for basecoating. Blend with a dry brush, and edge colors into one another with short choppy strokes to indicate short hairs. Don't over-work values to mud.

7 Blend shading and highlighting with smaller brushes than those with which you placed the paint. If the basecoating for a particular area was done with a no. 4, for example, the no. 2 will give you a cleaner highlight and muddy the paint less. In areas of medium-length hair, the no. 2 will work well; in areas of very very short, dense hair (above and below the eye, for example), you can stipple on lights with the round brush, and blend them with the flattened tip of the same brush.

As highlights are completed, use the small brights to "walk" light brush marks (Raw Sienna + White) into areas of medium and darker fur around the eye and on the forehead. These brush tracks suggest more depth and give more value changes in each area, which are necessary for good dimension.

6 Now we'll begin to add more depth by strengthening the darks, and lightening the whites. Use Burnt Sienna + Burnt Umber + Raw Umber to shade on top and within the Burnt Sienna + Raw Sienna areas. Use Raw Sienna + White to lighten the original Raw Sienna areas. Add highlight-white areas with cleaner White.

Fawn's Body & Spots

8 The body of the fawn is darkest on the back, a medium value centrally, and lightest as you reach the belly areas. Use the following values to base these areas, using a no. 4 bright. Go carefully around the spot shapes, taking care not to round them all into polka dots. The darkest areas, at the top of the back, are Burnt Umber + Black. Medium dark areas are Burnt Umber. Lighter medium values are Burnt Umber + Burnt Sienna + Raw Sienna. The lightest values on the body are Raw Sienna. As you apply the sparse color, let the chisel edge of the brush be parallel to the growth direction so that the initial lay of the coat is established.

9 Use the same brushes as those you used for basing to do the initial blending between values. Work first on lines where values meet, walking the brush back and forth across them to achieve a good value gradation. Apply the first shading color on top of the basecoat with Burnt Umber + Black. Apply the first highlights with Raw Sienna + White.

10 Blend the shading and highlighting with the growth direction, letting soft brush marks show between the spots to indicate the lay of the hair. Add spots with a no. 2 bright, using White + Raw Sienna. Spot color should edge just slightly into the dark surrounding values. Spot edges are not even, but rather have directional hair-like projections that reflect the growth direction.

11 Highlight the spots with a no. 2 bright and White + a tad of Raw Sienna. Add additional brush tracks to indicate the lay of the hair if needed.

Chipmunk's Tail & Body

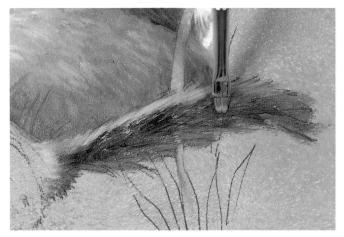

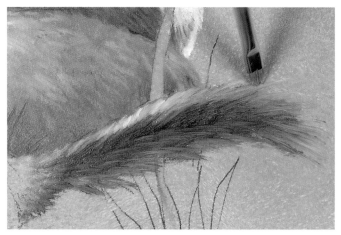

12 Base the darkest band on the chipmunk's tail with Burnt Umber + Black, using the no. 2 bright. Base the reddish band with Burnt Sienna + Burnt Umber. Base the lightest, topmost stripe with Raw Sienna + White.

13 With a dry chisel, pull short strokes on the lines where values meet, blending just enough between colors to give flow to the tail and keep values from appearing too separate. Highlight the lightest hair area with White + Raw Sienna. Add additional guard hairs with the same mix, but use a darker value in other areas of the tail. Note that the hairs actually do not lie along the length of the tail, but come out of the tail at an angle and are straight, not curved.

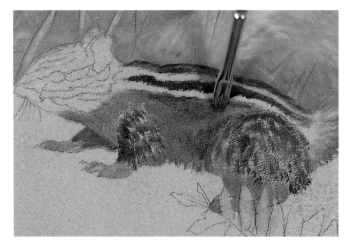

14 Base the feet with Burnt Sienna + Raw Sienna. Base the dark stripes with Burnt Umber + Black.

The body of the chipmunk is divided between areas of agouti, or salt-and-pepper gray hair, and areas of solid-color fur. Using a no. 2 or no. 4 in the ticked areas, basecoat with short, chisel-edge chop strokes of Black + Raw Umber, letting the strokes be more dense in areas of shadow and less so in areas where the ticked hairs will carry more light.

Base the solid-color dark areas in front of the hind leg and below the stripe area with Burnt Sienna + Burnt Umber, using the same brushes. Base the remainder of the side, belly and throat with Burnt Sienna + Raw Sienna.

15 With a dry brush, blend with short choppy strokes just a little on the lines where the various basecoat values meet. The solid-color fur values must gradate easily into the agouti areas, not remaining visually separate.

Now, using the no. 2 bright and White + Raw Umber, place the light value in the ticked hair areas. Then, with a little of the same color, walk the brush into the surrounding solid-color areas to add directional brush tracks and highlighting. Highlight the throat with Raw Sienna + White and the feet with Burnt Sienna + White. Add tiny toenails with Black, highlighted with Raw Sienna + White.

Add white stripes on the back with pure White, using a small brush. Note the mixed-up growth direction of these very short hairs. Some follow the length of the stripe, but many stick out at odd angles to the top and bottom.

Chipmunk's Head & Face

16 Base the eye-ring with Raw Sienna + White. With a clean liner brush, base the eye carefully and evenly with Black. With no. 0 bright, place a narrow dark line on the forehead and the eyeline in front of and behind the eye, using Black + Raw Umber. Narrow the eye-ring to the proper width where the colors meet. Base the nose with Black + Raw Umber.

The front half of the bottom facial stripe is based with Black + Raw Umber, while the back half is reddish, based with a mix of Burnt Umber + Burnt Sienna. Place a tad of this same rusty mix in front of the ear.

Outline the ears with White + Raw Umber. Fill with Black + Raw Umber in the darkest areas. Base the medium gray areas with Raw Umber + White. Blend just a little where the values meet.

Then, base a little fuzzy Raw Umber under the nose and on the chin, dragging it down to meet the Raw Sienna previously placed on the throat.

17 Lay in the short choppy strokes of Black + Raw Umber, which form the base for the ticked hairs on the forehead and the side of the face. Highlight the eye with a dot of White. Add the narrow white stripe on the face with a no. 0 bright and sparse paint. Again, the stripes are fuzzy and broken, with a random growth direction. Thin a bit of the Black + Raw Umber mix and, using a liner brush, add the whiskers, pulling from the whisker pad outward so the tips are the thinnest part.

18 With a small bright, lay in White sparsely to complete the ticked hair areas on the forehead and the side of the face. Highlight the nose with White + Raw Umber. With a dry brush, blend just a bit to connect the head to the neck to the body, so areas do not appear separate. Allow the painting to dry before adding the grasses and flowers that surround the animals.

Phlox

19 Place grass basecoats with Black + Sap Green. Use the same mix for the dark values on the fern leaflets. This stage can be quite rough, with color applied loosely and quickly with the no. 4 or no. 6 bright. Once the basecoats are applied, rub softly with cheesecloth to remove excess paint, and to give a dark green base for the detailed grasses and ferns to come.

20 Now replace the grasses with detailed strokes of Black + Sap Green for darker, distant values, and with Sap Green + Raw Sienna + White for the lighter values. Choose some of the more forward, more focal clusters, and highlight a few blades of grass with White + Sap Green + Raw Sienna.

Base the centers of the phlox with Alizarin Crimson + Winsor Violet using the no. 0 bright. Fill in the base of the petals with White. Now, base the tips of each petal sparsely with Alizarin Crimson + Winsor Violet, using a no. 2 bright.

21 Using the no. 2 bright, blend between values on the phlox petals. Rehighlight with White at the petal bases and blend to soften. With the liner brush, touch two tiny elongated dots of Cadmium Yellow Pale into each phlox center.

Finishing Touches

22 We want the phlox behind the fawn to appear faded. Use the same colors as used for the distant greenery and flowers, but apply them with very dry paint on sparsely loaded brushes. After all elements are applied, wipe most of the color off, using the cheesecloth pad, to soften the edges into the background. The center dots in the flowers may be added with a dirtier mix of the same colors as were used for flowers in the foreground. Do not rehighlight any of the white petal bases on the faded flowers.

Allow some variation of value and intensity within the distant grouping. To achieve the correct planes and perspective, a very few of the petals closer to the fawn as well as a few leaves and grass blades should be slightly stronger and more detailed than those further behind.

23 You may finish the grasses and allow them to dry before proceeding to the shadows under the animals, or you may do this step prior to applying grasses in this area.

Use Black + Raw Umber under the fawn and around the chipmunk to create strong shadows in those areas. Apply with a no. 6 or no. 8 bright.

24 Soften the shadow edges, pulling horizontally with a cheesecloth pad. If too much color is removed, strengthen with Black + Raw Umber again. Lay a narrow dark shadow right next to the fawn and under the chipmunk's feet to anchor them to the surface.

Additional depth can be built in areas of the grass clusters by adding similar shadows and then softening with cheesecloth.

Sherry C. Nelson

Cottontail Rabbit & Butterfly

The beautiful little Desert Cottontail takes sanctuary here, in this scene from my garden. Nibbling at the bird seed, drinking from the water drip and playing hide-and-go-seek amongst the irises, this garden critter is always alert and in touch with everything that goes on around him.

The beautiful Arizona sister butterfly is a common one in the yard. It's not unusual to see the rabbits, birds and even deer take notice of this butterfly's bouncy flight, watching as it sips the nectar from favorite blooms.

Irises carry a toxin in the rhizome that makes them unpalatable to deer, rabbits and javelinas. We enjoy this beautiful bloom all the more because it is often the only flower we can successfully grow!

Color Mixes

Use these swatches when mixing oils or matching to other paint mediums.

Black + Raw Umber	Raw Sienna + White	Black + Raw Umber	White + Black + Raw Umber
White + Raw Sienna + Raw Umber	Raw Sienna + Raw Umber + White	Black + Sap Green	Sap Green + Raw Sienna + White
Burnt Sienna + White	White + Raw Sienna	Winsor Violet + Raw Sienna + tad of White	Winsor Violet + Raw Sienna
Cadmium Yellow Pale + White	White + Sap Green + Raw Sienna	Burnt Sienna + Winsor Red + Cadmium Yellow Pale	White + Black

Line Drawing

Transfer this line drawing to the prepared
background using dark graphite paper. Be
very accurate when transferring the eye and
facial features of the rabbit and the spots
and detail on the butterfly. Don't let fur
areas "grow" outside the drawing, and also
make sure flower shapes are correct.

This pattern may be hand-traced or photocopied for personal use only. Enlarge at 143%
to bring it up to full size.

Materials & Reference Photos

To paint the background, you'll need:

- Hardboard (Masonite) panel, 14" x 11" x ⅛"
  (36cm x 28cm x 3mm)
- Sponge roller
- Acrylic paints by Delta Ceramcoat
  English Yew Green
  Rainforest Green
  Cactus Green
  Trail Tan
- Paper towels
- Protected work surface
- 320-grit wet/dry sandpaper
- Krylon Matte Finish no. 1311

To paint the Desert Cottontail and Arizona Sister Butterfly, you'll need:

- Oil paints
  Ivory Black
  Titanium White
  Raw Sienna
  Raw Umber
  Burnt Sienna
  Sap Green
  Cadmium Yellow Pale
  Winsor Red
  Windsor Violet
- Brushes
  nos. 0, 2, 4, 6 and 8 red sable short brights
  no. 0 red sable liner
- Odoriess thinner
- Cobalt drier (optional)
- Palette knife
- Paper towels
- Disposable palette for oils
- Dark graphite paper
- Tracing paper
- Ballpoint pen
- Cheesecloth

Several years ago, we found an injured bunny alongside the road. Naturally, we brought her home to the Intensive Care Unit. During her weeks of recovery we took the opportunity to take pictures—a lot of them. My favorite reference for this painting is this shot of her in the big flower bed in front, peeking over the top with a natural curiosity about her new surroundings. As soon as I saw this picture, my mind began working on ways it could be combined with other elements to tell the story of how the world looks from a cottontail's point of view.

PHOTOS BY DEBORAH A. GALLOWAY

We also picked up this injured Arizona Sister butterfly along the road—and took an imprompu shot on the dashboard of the car. Opportunities for reference photography can arise at odd times, and you have to be ready to take quick advantage of them. You never know when something you discover may offer a once-in-a-lifetime photo. Deb almost never steps out the door without a camera in hand.

Reference Photos & Background

With more than sixty-five varieties of iris in the yard, they are a favorite photographic subject as well. When shooting flowers, be sure to take photos of their leaves and buds, as well as the full-blown flowers themselves. I like to have a series of shots over several days: as the bud first forms, as it develops more fully, as it begins to show a bit of color and so forth. Then you have the opportunity to include those natural stages of growth in a painting—all the better to tell a story with your design.

PHOTOS BY DEBORAH A. GALLOWAY

1 Review chapter 2, Painting Backgrounds, before beginning. Basecoat the Masonite panel with Cactus Green and allow it to dry. Sand smooth.

Then apply colors as shown on the color-placement diagram, blending with the sponge roller between each value. When the three values are nicely gradated, drizzle a little Trail Tan onto the upper third of the surface and blend it into the Cactus Green, about where the x's appear on the diagram. The roller allows you to leave the surface either a little underblended or blended quite smoothly. I believe the former—the out-of-focus, splotchy look—makes the painting more interesting. When dry, sand smooth. Finally, spray with Krylon Matte Finish no. 1311.

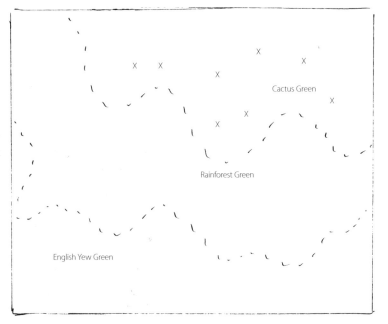

Cactus Green

Rainforest Green

English Yew Green

Diagram for Color Placement

X = Trail Tan

Cottontail's Eye

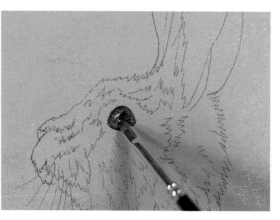

2 Using the liner, place a narrow line of Black inside the iris of the eye to the outer edge. Then fill in the remainder of the iris with Raw Umber.

3 With a clean, small bright, fill in the pupil with pure Black.

4 Using the liner brush, come around the iris from nine o'clock to two o'clock with a line of Black + Raw Umber. Extend this color into the forward corner in front of the eye. Add the highlight dot with the liner brush on the line between the pupil and the iris at eleven o'clock. Then lay on short fur areas around the eye with Raw Sienna + White.

5 Base the nosepad with Burnt Sienna + White. Base Raw Sienna + White around the nose, on the whisker pad. Fill in the facial areas as shown with Raw Sienna. These areas will act as warm tones underlying the gray fur of the face and neck. Highlight the fur around the eyes with White + a tad of Raw Sienna using a no. 0 bright.

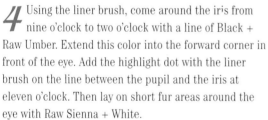

6 Blend the highlight on the fur around the eyes with the growth direction, using a dry no. 0 bright. Highlight the nosepad with a very light value of White + a little Burnt Sienna. Add a Raw Sienna basecoat at the nape of the neck.

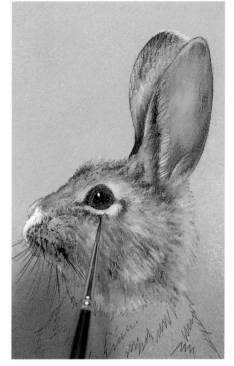

7 Base the inner ear with Burnt Sienna along the left side, Raw Sienna in the central area, and Raw Umber as shading where shown, allowing the darker values to form a rough patch at the base of the ear and around the right edge.

Begin to place a basecoat of strokes of Black + Raw Umber where shown, noticing that some will come on top and into the edges of the Raw Sienna areas. The dark strokes may be clustered and become closer together in areas where darker shadows occur (as in the ear area). Notice how the pattern of choppy, chisel-edge marks reflects the changes in the hair length in different areas. It also reflects the lay of the fur and its pattern as it follows the shape of the head, neck and outside of the ears.

8 Here I've added overstrokes with a dirty brush + White to fill in spaces between the choppy, dark-mix strokes. High areas of contour are becoming obvious, and the addition of the pale gray mix begins to give our rabbit its characteristic ticked gray coat. Use a bit of additional White + Raw Sienna around the eyes for final highlights and to emphasize the eye shape correctly. Highlight with Burnt Sienna + White inside the ear with choppy strokes. Add additional final light strokes on the whisker pad, ear edges, and contour areas of the face.

9 Using a liner brush and Black + Raw Umber, create the final detail of dark spots for the whisker bases and the dark shading around the eye and at the base of the ears. Thin this mix to do the whiskers, using the liner. Using White + Raw Sienna on the liner, fluff out the small hairs on the chin, the edges of the nape and the forehead to soften the hard edges of the animal and to make it look fuzzy and soft. Last of all, additional white highlights can be added with the liner to build more texture in the lightest fur areas and next to the nose.

10 Begin basecoating the warm areas of the body with choppy strokes of Raw Sienna, using a no. 4 bright. On the very front of the legs, where they catch the most light, use Raw Sienna + White. Then begin adding the dark, choppy basecoating for the ticked hair areas. When you meet the Raw Sienna patches, chop into the edges to connect the fur areas. The ticked partial basecoat of Black + Raw Umber is where you begin to define shadow areas by making strokes closer together. It is also where you begin to create form and contour by carefully watching growth direction and the lay of the fur. Study the example here and notice how, even at this early stage, the form and shape of the rabbit become evident.

11 Wipe the brush dry, and load it with White, pulling color into a pale gray loading zone. Begin adding the light values into the ticked hairs, pulling perhaps eight to ten strokes, and then reloading. Make the hair strokes the correct length for the fur in each area, and be sure to follow the growth direction and lay of the fur as you did for the dark strokes. Highlight the legs with strokes in a lighter value of Raw Sienna + White. Shade the bottoms of the feet and the far front leg in the shadow area with short strokes of Raw Umber.

12 Finalize the ticking and solid-color fur areas with any additional white highlights or shading needed. Fluff the short guard hairs from the edge of the body to soften the shape on the legs, chest and back.

Cottontail's Lower Body & Iris

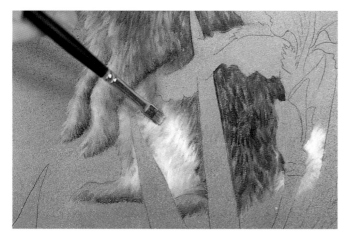

13 The lower body is done much the same. Use choppy strokes of Black + Raw Umber in ticked areas of the fur. Base the belly with strokes of White + Raw Sienna + Raw Umber in a very pale value. Place short strokes of Raw Sienna on top of the hind feet and of Raw Umber for the shadowy pad of each foot. Base the tail with the mix used on the belly.

14 Use White + Raw Umber strokes to complete the ticked fur areas. Highlight the belly and tail with strokes of clean White. Accent the belly with Raw Sienna and blend softly. Highlight the tops of the feet with Raw Sienna + White.

15 Use a no. 4 bright to base the dark area in the falls (bottom iris petals) with Winsor Violet + Raw Sienna + White. Base the light value of the falls with Raw Sienna + White.

Base the dark value in each standard (upright petal) with Raw Sienna + White. Base the light value with White.

Use color sparsely and let your strokes follow the natural growth direction of the petal.

16 Using the chisel edge of a very dry brush, blend between the values in both standards and falls, creating a value gradation between the original values. Then place the white highlights on both standards and falls. Shade with Raw Umber on the standards and with Winsor Violet + Raw Sienna on the falls.

Iris Petals & Leaves

17 Blend the inner edges of the highlights in the growth direction of each petal. Use additional White if needed to create more emphasis and suggestion of folds and ridges. Soften the shading as well, blending with the growth. Detail the central vein in the largest standard with White and with Sap Green + Black.

Base the beards with Cadmium Yellow Pale + White. Accent the base of each beard with Burnt Sienna + Winsor Red + Cadmium Yellow Pale. See the finished painting for a good look at this detail.

Base the stems with Sap Green + Black. Base the darker values on the calyxes with Raw Umber and the lighter values with Raw Sienna + Raw Umber + White. Then, base the leaves with darker values, using Sap Green + Black.

18 Base the remaining areas of the leaves with lighter values of Sap Green + Raw Sienna + White. Highlight the stems with the same light green mix, pulling a line down the center of the stem and softening edges to round.

Blend the individual sections of the calyxes, and then shade with Raw Umber and highlight with Raw Sienna + more White than was used in the base mix.

Base the bud with the iris mixes: Winsor Violet + Raw Sienna + White for the dark value and Raw Sienna + White for the lighter value.

19 Blend between values on the leaves, pulling the brush lengthwise. The larger the leaf, the larger the brush you should use. The one shown here can be comfortably blended with a no. 6. Using Sap Green + Raw Sienna + more White, lay on leaf highlights.

Blend the bud with short strokes across the bud, not lengthwise, to indicate how the petals are wrapped around the bud. Add highlights with White.

20 Blend the leaf highlights, pulling lightly along the length of the leaf. Using a light-value green mix, you may add a soft central vein if desired. Blend highlights on the bud, again showing a crosswise growth direction.

Arizona Sister Butterfly

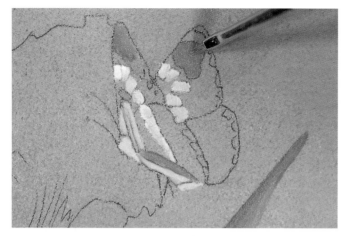

21 Using the no. 0 liner, base in the orange spots on the butterfly using Burnt Sienna + Winsor Red + Cadmium Yellow Pale. Base the white spots with a very light mix of White + Raw Sienna. Base the elongated stripes and the head of the butterfly with a cool mix of White + Black.

22 Base around all spots precisely and carefully, using Raw Umber + Black. Use the no. 2 bright in larger areas and the no. 0 bright in very tight sections. Use the same dark mix to add separation lines between sections. Use the chisel edge to set them in; do not pull them between spots. Setting the lines with repeated taps of the chisel gives the proper fuzzy texture to the lines and prevents muddying, which may occur if the stroke is pulled.

23 Thin Black + Raw Umber with odorless thinner and use a liner brush to apply the fine veining in the wings, legs and antennae. Touch on dots of Raw Sienna + White for the markings along the edge of the wing. Highlight the orange sections with the same mix.

24 Basecoat the standards on the left iris, using Raw Sienna + White for the dark value and White + a little Raw Sienna for the lighter value. For the falls, use Winsor Violet + Raw Sienna for the dark value and Raw Sienna + White for the light value.

Final Touches

26 Let the painting dry, then complete the following steps. Place the shadows under the rabbit with Raw Umber + Black.

Make a mix of Raw Umber + Sap Green and thin with odorless thinner. Use a palette knife to place scrapes of this color on the surface where additional depth is desired, such as at the base of the clusters of iris leaves, and at the edges of the surface for more interest.

25 Blend the standards and falls with the growth direction appropriate for each petal. Apply the white highlights on the standards, and shade to give dimension with Raw Umber + White. Add white highlights on the falls. Add the beards with Cadmium Yellow Pale + White. Accent at the base of each beard with a little of the orange mix from the butterfly's spots. See the finished painting for these final steps.

27 Using a soft pad of cheesecloth, blend the shadows under the rabbit horizontally and soften the edges until they fade away. Deepen the color right under the rabbit with Black to create a resting shadow to anchor the animal to the surface. Soften the very edge of that with the cheesecloth, too. Then use the cheesecloth to blend and soften the antiquing glaze in a soft, out-of-focus pattern.

Finally, thin the antiquing mix a bit more and add the very faint "shadow" leaves in the background behind the rabbit. If these get a bit too heavy, simply use the cheesecloth pad to remove some paint and soften them so they stay in the background.

Sherry C. Nelson

Kitten and Baby Chick

T he little chick is a banty Buff Cochin, one of dozens that my small garden flock of chickens hatched over the years. They fascinated me, with their fit-in-the-palm-of-your-hand size and little "bedroom-slipper" feet—fluffy feathers covering their toes from the moment of hatching. But I worried about our city-bred house cats, new to the idea of farm critters, who occasionally accompanied me to the chicken yard for chores. Would they bother the babies? Never did, not once. The cats observed and studied the little chicks with great interest and eventually came to take an almost maternal attitude, at times acting very protective. As always, I was intrigued by the intricate and complex interactions between very different creatures in which, it seems, there's always a story to tell.

Color Mixes

Use these swatches when mixing oils or matching to other paint mediums.

Black + Raw Umber	White + Raw Umber + Black	Burnt Sienna + Raw Umber	Raw Sienna + White	Cadmium Yellow Pale + Raw Sienna
Cadmium Yellow Pale + White	French Ultramarine + White	White + Cadmium Yellow Pale + Raw Sienna	Burnt Sienna + Winsor Red + Cadmium Yellow Pale	French Ultramarine + Black + White
White + French Ultramarine + Black	Raw Sienna + Raw Umber	Sap Green + Black	Sap Green + Raw Sienna + White	White + Raw Sienna + Sap Green
Raw Umber + White	Burnt Sienna + White	Burnt Sienna + Raw Sienna + Raw Umber		

Line Drawing

Transfer this design to the pre-pared background using dark graphite paper. Be very accurate when transferring the eyes, facial features, feathers and fur. The lines of the scoop and the flowers need a careful hand too.

This pattern may be hand-traced or photocopied for personal use only. Enlarge at 147% to bring it up to full size.

Materials & Reference Photos

To paint the background, you'll need:

- Hardboard (Masonite) panel, 14" x 11" x ⅛"
  (36cm x 28cm x 3mm)
- Sponge roller
- Acrylic paints by Delta Ceramcoat
  - Silver Pine
  - Cactus Green
  - Rainforest Green
  - Cadet Grey
- Paper towels
- Protected work surface
- 320-grit wet/dry sandpaper
- Krylon Matte Finish no. 1311

To paint the Kitten and Baby Chick, you'll need:

- Oil paints
  - Ivory Black
  - Titanium White
  - Raw Sienna
  - Raw Umber
  - Burnt Sienna
  - Sap Green
  - Cadmium Yellow Pale
  - Winsor Red
  - French Ultramarine
- Brushes
  - nos. 0, 2, 4, 6 and 8 red sable short brights
  - no. 0 red sable liner
- Odorless thinner
- Cobalt drier (optional)
- Palette knife
- Paper towels
- Disposable palette for oils
- Dark graphite paper
- Tracing paper
- Ballpoint pen
- Cheesecloth
- Stylus

Kittens aren't always easy to find when you need some fresh, exciting photos. So we've learned to take advantage of a wonderful resource: our local animal shelter. For a small donation, the caring folks there let us photograph the kittens and puppies and we get the added bonus of a delightful afternoon, playing with all the babies. We take props with us—strings to pull, a catnip mouse and a snack or two—and settle in to see if we can turn the action-filled antics into some good references for paintings that tell a story.

We always seemed to have new baby chicks in the early spring. This photo graced our Easter cards one year, and was kept for a photo reference. The low angle shot, plus the chick standing in Easter basket "grass" made the switch to the scoop and a handful of barnyard straw a natural one. Be creative in your approach to photography. Try to think of all the myriad of possibilities and then shoot with the creature's point of view in mind.

Filler was needed to balance the main attractions, and the yellow jonquils seemed perfect with the yellow kitten and chick. Repetition of color in the main elements leads the eye through the painting while giving the odd object, such as the scoop, additional interest. Again, get down low; don't take flower photos (or critters, either) from a "people" point of view.

PHOTOS BY DEBORAH A. GALLOWAY

Eye Demo & Preparing Background

The Eyes Have It!

KITTEN'S
EYES

Define pupil and iris.

Dark areas are natural shadow.

Fur base is added.

Strong lights make fur look thick.

Hairs soften edge of eyes.

Short hairs build depth, look plush, not hairy.

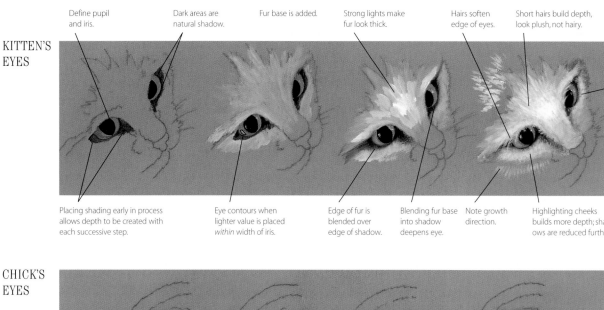

Addition of light "sinks" eyes more, blends to shadow.

Placing shading early in process allows depth to be created with each successive step.

Eye contours when lighter value is placed *within* width of iris.

Edge of fur is blended over edge of shadow.

Blending fur base into shadow deepens eye.

Note growth direction.

Highlighting cheeks builds more depth; shadows are reduced further.

CHICK'S
EYES

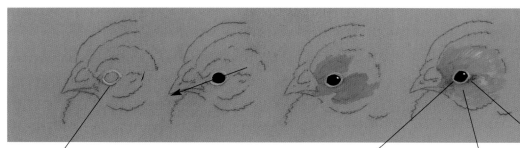

Basic and shading colors should touch eyering, break and blend into it and narrow its width

Place eye-ring first.

Fill in pupil carefully, aligning eye shape to position in head.

Fill in basic feather colors.

Edge of eye-ring should be broken, uneven.

First highlight color

Shading

1 Review chapter 2, Painting Backgrounds, before beginning. Basecoat the Masonite panel with Silver Pine. Let dry, sand and re-basecoat. While it's wet, drizzle some Cactus Green on the upper part of the surface and Rainforest Green on the lower half. Use the same roller to blend and connect color areas and to soften into the background. Finally, on the upper areas of the surface, add a little Cadet Grey and roll to blend into the greens for a combination highlight and intensity control. Let dry, then sand smooth. Spray with matte finish.

Wooden Scoop

2 Begin by laying in the dark values of wood graining on the handle and back of the scoop. Use Black + Raw Umber, working the chisel of the no. 4 or 6 brush to create the streaked look. Base the remainder of the areas with White + Raw Umber, in a soft medium-light value of gray. Base the end of the handle where it penetrates the back of the scoop with Black + Raw Umber in the darkest areas and a bit of Raw Sienna in the lighter central area.

3 Using a dry chisel edge, blend between the dark and light values following the wood grain. Add some rusty discolored areas with a mix of Burnt Sienna + Raw Sienna. Blend into surrounding base colors just a bit. Finally, pick up a little Black + Raw Umber on a no. 2 bright, and lay in some detailed, dark values of wood graining. If certain areas appear a bit heavy-handed, just pat them a bit with the cheesecloth to soften into the background colors.

4 The metal sides of the scoop are very rough and pitted and have some rusty areas as well as some white scaling, all of which makes it look old. Use Black for the darkest values, Black + French Ultramarine + White for the medium areas, and a lighter value of the medium mix for the lightest areas on the sides. Base the bottom of the scoop roughly and very sparsely with Raw Sienna + Raw Umber.

5 Blend between the value areas very roughly using a no. 6 bright. Then thin a little Black, and with the liner brush, lay in areas of squiggles to indicate pitted, irregular areas. Then repeat this process with thinned White, with the same brush as shown here. Add a few areas of uneven, splotchy Raw Sienna + Burnt Sienna for accent.

6 Pat the areas of thinned Black and White with the cheesecloth pad to soften. Just pushing on the damp paint a little presses it into the basecoat and makes the additions appear much more realistic than they would otherwise.

Baby Chick

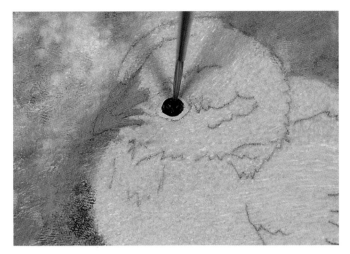

7 Base the chick's beak with Raw Sienna + Burnt Sienna. Base the eye-ring with Raw Sienna + White, using the liner brush. Rinse the liner brush in thinner, and blot on a paper towel. Load the tip in pure Black and fill in the eye, making a clean, sharp edge where it meets the eye-ring.

8 With the liner brush, add a tiny highlight dot in the eye. Using a no. 2 bright, highlight the beak as shown using Raw Sienna + White. Base in the remaining colors on the head, using Raw Sienna + Burnt Sienna for the darkest value; Raw Sienna adjacent to the dark mix as a buffer; and Cadmium Yellow Pale + Raw Sienna for the more yellow areas. As each different color touches the eye-ring, begin the process of narrowing it to a more realistic size and shape.

9 Blend between values using short choppy strokes of the no. 2 bright. Establish the initial growth direction and the suggestion of "fluff" at this early stage and it will be easier to get the round contoured form of the chick later on.

Begin highlighting with Raw Sienna + White, using the no. 2 bright. Apply highlights with strokes that follow the growth direction of the feathers, then wipe the brush dry and blend in the same manner, softening the strongest highlights a bit into the basecoat colors to subdue them. When all initial lights are added, you may consider additional, lighter whites for final fluff.

Shade within and at the base of the beak, and in front of and behind the eye with Raw Umber, to set the eye and to control the intensity of the stronger yellow tones.

Chick & Straw

10 Apply basecoat colors very sparsely on the chick's body, using a no. 2 or 4 bright. Dark values are Raw Sienna + Burnt Sienna; the medium value is Raw Sienna; and the lightest areas are Raw Sienna + White, and White + Raw Sienna, in a slightly lighter value. Establish the initial growth direction, and then keep your brush strokes short to indicate the shorter, downy feathers of the chick.

11 Wipe dry the brushes used for basecoating and begin to blend between the different value areas. Work especially on lines where values meet to create good value gradations that help the different shadow and light areas on the body to create form and dimension. Fluff the edges of the chick a little to break up outlines.

Now begin highlighting as you did on the head, using Raw Sienna + White first, chopping color in the growth direction with the chisel edge of a no. 2 bright. Notice the cleaner white that appears on the breast and wing feathers; for those areas use the same mix plus a little more White.

12 Blend the highlights a little to soften. Fluff on any final lights needed with the same mix and a light touch. Add White + Cadmium Yellow Pale accents to brighten where needed.

Lay in the basecoat colors for the straw under and around the chick and inside the old scoop. Use each color by turn, beginning with the darker values and working to the light: Raw Umber, Raw Sienna and finally, Raw Sienna + White for the lightest values. Here and there, add a bit of Burnt Sienna to warm. Pull a few strokes of straw over the feet, leaving just a little feathering to show. Add Burnt Sienna toenails on the left foot, and then highlight them with just a touch of Burnt Sienna + White.

Daffodils

13 Begin to basecoat the leaves and stems of the daffodils, using Black + Sap Green for the dark values and Sap Green + Raw Sienna + White for the lighter value along the sides of the leaves. For the 2 or 3 inches of the tips of the leaves, use French Ultramarine + White for the lighter value.

The daffodil petals are based with White + Cadmium Yellow Pale + Raw Sienna. Base the center trumpet with Sap Green + Black at the very center; use the pale petal mix around the green center; then a band of Raw Sienna; and finally edge the trumpet with the bright orangey-red mix of Winsor Red + Cadmium Yellow Pale + Burnt Sienna.

With flowers, the trick is to keep the basecoat colors very dry; apply them sparsely; and don't let the colors muddy together before you are ready to blend. Flowers naturally appear rather translucent, and heavy paint can overwhelm.

14 Blend the leaves lengthwise with a dry no. 6 bright. Lay on highlight areas on the leaves and stems with White + Sap Green + Raw Sienna.

Using a dry chisel edge, blend between the values on the trumpets. Begin by connecting the dark green centers to the surrounding light value. Do not pull the green out, but rather just let the colors interlock a bit to break up the line between the values.

With the chisel, blend with the growth, between the edge of the light value and the Raw Sienna. Finally, by just notching a bit into the orange edge, break it into the Raw Sienna band to soften and break up the line between the colors.

Shade under the overlapping edges of the petals with Raw Umber + White. Add highlights where shown on the petals.

15 Blend leaf highlights smoothly with the length of each leaf. Add soft, light central veining.

Blend the highlights on the petals with the chisel, carefully shaping the growth direction of each petal as you work. You may wish to rehighlight with White one more time, and reblend to build more dramatic spark in a few dominant petals.

Add the stamens inside the trumpets, basing first with Raw Sienna and then highlighting with Cadmium Yellow Pale. Base the calyxes with Raw Sienna. Highlight with the dirty brush + White.

Kitten

16 Base the irises of the kitten's eyes with French Ultramarine +White. Lay a narrow band around the irises using Raw Umber. Widen the shading at the corners of the eyes. Scruff in dry, sparse Raw Umber next to the nose and to define the mouth area. Base the nosepad with Burnt Sienna. Place Burnt Sienna and Burnt Sienna + White inside the ears.

17 Highlight the iris with dirty white, blending the light to soften a bit as it curves around the eye. Using a clean no. 0 bright, base the pupils with Black, creating a clean edge next to the iris. Add a highlight dot with the liner brush.

Highlight the nosepad with Burnt Sienna + White. Highlight inside the ears with White + a tad of Burnt Sienna, and blend with the growth direction to indicate the longer hairs inside the ears.

Base the face, muzzle, neck ruff and edges of ears with White. Dark areas behind the ears and on top of the head are Raw Sienna + Raw Umber; medium values are Raw Sienna + Burnt Sienna + Raw Umber, and are found in a line from the corners of the eyes, and on the forehead to indicate the tabby markings. The lightest value of the yellow fur areas is Raw Sienna.

18 Using a small dry bright, blend between the dark, medium and light values of the yellow fur until the growth direction and hair length are somewhat established and colors no longer appear separate.

Lay on initial highlights with Raw Sienna + White, concentrating them on the forehead and top of the nose, under the eyes, on the cheek and around the edges of the ears. They can be applied in the areas of the head where hairs are longer using a small bright. Where hair is dense and short, as on the nose and under the eyes, the White can be stippled on using a liner brush. This gives a thicker coat of paint, and adds to the plush look of the fur.

19 With a dry no. 2 bright, blend the light values just enough to soften and fluff. Thin some White and use the liner brush to pull out white ear hairs and whiskers. Add a few guard hairs at the edges of the head and back of neck to soften the outline of the body, but don't overdo.

20 Base the body and legs of the kitten using Raw Sienna + Raw Umber for the darker values; Raw Sienna for the medium value; and White for the lightest fur on the legs and underbelly. Use a no. 2 or 4 bright on the short leg hairs and a no. 4 bright for the longer back hairs. Watch growth direction, especially on the legs, where the short hairs often fluff out perpendicularly to the edge of the leg rather than following the line of the leg. Lay in Raw Umber for the dark value of the wood plank under the kitten, and Raw Sienna for the medium value.

21 Use dry chisel edges to blend between fur values, and to create correct growth direction and hair lengths on all areas of the body. Lay on strong highlights on the front of the legs with White and fluff with growth direction.

Blend values on the plank with the chisel edge following the direction of the wood grain. Graining on the plank should be less strong than that on the more important scoop. Allow the painting to dry before continuing.

22 When working with whites, it's easiest to build the really sparky, strong lights on a dry surface. Study this full shot to find the additional white added to the kitten's chest and front of the legs, and on the flower petals. Place the lights as shown, then blend with a dry chisel. If the color does not move easily, simply rub a bit with cheesecloth.

Final guard hairs may also be added at this point, using very, very thin Raw Sienna + White and applied sparingly with the liner brush. Remember, it takes only a few of these longer, more dramatic hairs to make the kitten appear soft and fluffy. Do not overdo.

23 I like to do the shadows under objects in a painting at this point too, when the surface is dry and I can work into tight areas more easily without disturbing wet paint.

Lay on shadows under the daffodils, the leaves, and under the scoop using Raw Umber. Lay on a bit generously, then blend color at the edges to soften using a pad of cheesecloth. Now go back, and right under the bottom edge of the scoop and in the deepest dark areas of shadow under the flowers and leaves, add a bit of Black + Raw Umber shadow to "set down" the objects more securely on the surface. Edges may again be blended with cheesecloth to soften if necessary.

24 Normally at this point I'm finished with the painting. But in this instance, I was still dissatisfied with the kitten's eyes, which didn't "track" to the chick just right. The dry surface makes adjustments very simple and risk free; anything you choose to change can be removed if it doesn't work out.

The location of the pupil in the eye seemed to be the problem. With a little Black, I simply extended it to the bottom of the eye, immediately making the kitten appear to be looking downward. Some small additional highlights also helped make the eyes softer.

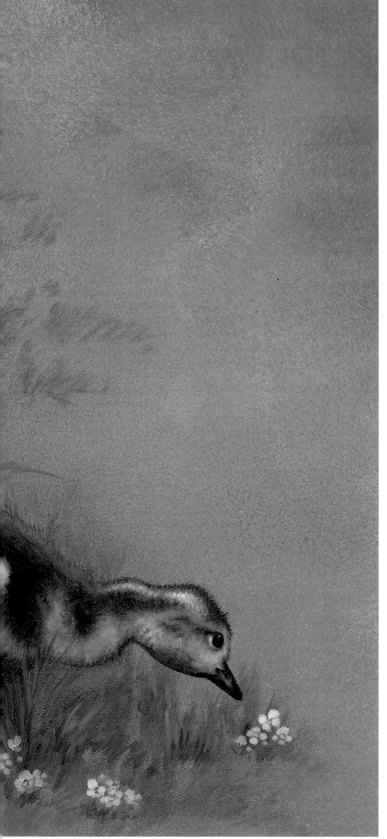

Puppy & the Gosling

Family pets are just as much a part of the garden scene as the wild animals. On occasion, they cross paths, as in this delightful encounter between the pup and the gosling.

Canada geese delight in tender grasses and thus take advantage of lawns and gardens, becoming a part of the suburban fauna in many areas. So it's not too hard to imagine this meeting, with the puppy trying to decide whether to chase or to lay low, as the little gosling calmly munches along. The unseen presence, of course, is the mother goose, who will come out of nowhere to defend her little ones, and to give a quick lesson to a nosy pup.

Color Mixes

Use these swatches when mixing oils or matching to other paint mediums.

Raw Sienna + White	Black + Raw Umber	Raw Sienna + Cadmium Yellow Pale + White	Burnt Sienna + White
White + Raw Sienna	Black + Sap Green	Purple Madder Alizarin + Raw Sienna + White	Purple Madder Alizarin + Raw Sienna + more White
Purple Madder Alizarin + Raw Sienna	White + Black + Raw Umber	Burnt Sienna + Raw Umber	Black + Raw Umber + White
Sap Green + Raw Sienna + White	Sap Green + Raw Sienna + more White	Cadmium Yellow Pale + White	Cadmium Yellow Pale + Raw Sienna

Line Drawing

Transfer this line drawing to the prepared background using dark graphite paper. Be very accurate when transferring the puppy's and gosling's eyes and other features, as well the the length and lie of the pup's fur and the gosling's fluffy down. Don't let the transfer "grow" outside of the pattern lines.

This pattern may be hand-traced or photocopied for personal use only. Enlarge at 153% to bring it up to full size.

Materials & Reference Photos

To paint the background, you'll need:

- Hardboard (Masonite) panel, 14" x 11" x ⅛" (36cm x 28cm x 3mm)
- Sponge roller
- Acrylic paints by Delta Ceramcoat
    Moss Green
    Seminole Green
    Gamal Green
    Rainforest Green
- Paper towels
- Protected work surface
- 320-grit wet/dry sandpaper
- Krylon Matte Finish no. 1311

To paint the Puppy and the Gosling, you'll need:

- Oil paints
    Ivory Black
    Titanium White
    Raw Sienna
    Raw Umber
    Burnt Sienna
    Sap Green
    Cadmium Yellow Pale
    Alizarin Crimson
    Purple Madder Alizarin
- Brushes
    nos. 0, 2, 4, 6 and 8 red sable short brights
    no. 0 red sable liner
- Odorless thinner
- Cobalt drier (optional)
- Palette knife
- Paper towels
- Disposable palette for oils
- Dark graphite paper
- Tracing paper
- Ballpoint pen
- Cheesecloth

Here's the inspiration for the painting: Daisy, a friend's cockapoo playing on the living room rug. It's also an example of why it pays to get down on your hands and knees (or belly!) when shooting animals. The eye-to-eye contact on the animal's level is only possible in this painting because the camera was low when the photos were taken.

PHOTO BY DEBORAH A. GALLOWAY

Here's the reference shot for the little gosling. Nearby were several more goslings, with the adult geese watching over them. Usually it's best when photographing for reference to shoot individual animals close-up, by themselves, rather than many in a single photo at a greater distance. In general, the closer the shot, the more information you will have for fur, eyes and the other essentials you need to see well to make your painting realistic.

PHOTO BY ARTHUR MORRIS

Reference Photos & First Steps

This container of flowers was shot in a nursery setting. As soon as I saw it, the many possibilities for inclusion in a painting, whether in whole or in part, became evident. I ended up using only a portion of it for the puppy to hide behind, but it's effective nonetheless. And by the way, always ask permission to take photos in a place of business before you set up your gear. We take time to explain the hows and whys of decorative painting to the business owner, and have made many friends along the way. In the more distant shot, the detail of the alyssum is difficult to discern; hence the closeup shot (below right) for a better understanding of the flower's structure and more inspiration for the painting itself.

PHOTOS BY DEBORAH A. GALLOWAY

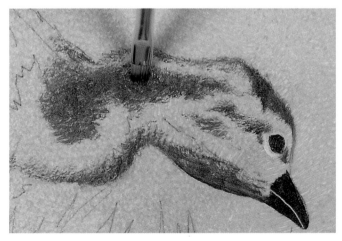

1 Review chapter 2, Painting Backgrounds, before beginning. Basecoat the Masonite panel with Moss Green, using a sponge roller. Let dry, sand and re-basecoat. While it's wet, drizzle some Rainforest Green in the central area of the surface. Blend it to a splotchy effect, moving some around to other areas, using the same sponge roller. Now, in areas where shadows will be most evident, such as next to and in front of the container, under the pup and in the foreground in front of the gosling, drizzle a little Seminole Green and use the roller to blend it in. Deepen those areas with Gamal Green to add another value. Roll the roller firmly on paper toweling between colors, and before final blending. Allow to dry, then sand. Spray the panel with a matte finishing spray.

2 Base the gosling's eye-ring with Raw Sienna + White using the liner brush. Rinse the brush in thinner, blot on a paper towel and load in clean Black. Fill in the eye carefully and precisely. Base the beak with Black + Raw Umber, using a no. 2 bright.

Fuzz in dark areas as shown using Raw Umber + a little Black on a no. 4 bright.

Gosling

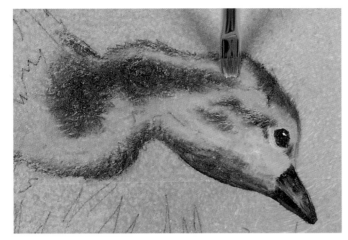

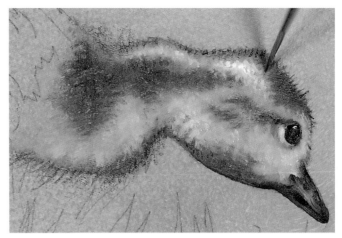

3 Highlight the eye with a dot of White. Highlight the beak with White + Raw Umber, applied with a small bright. Fill in the remainder of the head and neck area with Raw Sienna + a little White. Strokes can be chopped onto the surface to follow growth direction at this early stage, but should be very short, since the down on the gosling is almost non-directional in some areas.

4 Touch in short directional strokes with a no. 2 bright where values meet. Break the edges of dark and light together. Highlight with additional Raw Sienna + White, with Raw Sienna + Cadmium Yellow Pale + White, and also give these light areas the proper direction by using short choppy strokes of the chisel edge.

For final detailing, use a liner brush and pull fine lines of slightly thinned (with odorless thinner) Raw Umber + Black at the edges of the body and head to give a more fluffy appearance and to break up the line of the body. Interestingly, many of these fuzzy areas stick straight out from the body.

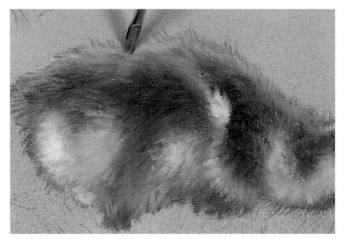

5 Using a no. 4 bright, begin laying in the downy areas of the body with slightly longer strokes using Black + Raw Umber for dark areas and Raw Sienna + White for the lighter values. Connect the dark and light areas with choppy strokes that fall over the junction of values and walk back and forth across it. It's a mistake to let color areas remain too separate, since that may reduce the appearance of the natural contours of the body.

6 Add final highlighting with White + Raw Sienna, and then a little plain White, chopping on strokes in the lightest areas with a no. 2 bright. Add some Raw Sienna accent within the lighter values on the body. Finally, thin some White + Black + Raw Umber and apply fine guard hairs, fluff and detail. Don't forget to break up edges of the body. Be careful though, this is how the painted areas "grow" beyond the design. We don't want to turn this gosling into a goose!

Puppy

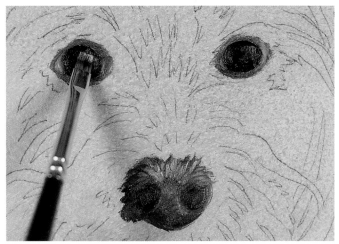

7 Base the pup's eye-rings with Raw Umber. Fill in the eyes with pure, clean Black. Base the nostrils with Black. Base the nosepad with a very dark gray made with Black + Raw Umber + a bit of White. Base the top of the nose with Burnt Sienna + Raw Umber.

8 Highlight the nosepad with a very grayed white, being careful not to get it too light. Choppy strokes of the no. 2 bright loaded with Raw Sienna + White are used to highlight the reddish top of the the nose. Notice the fan-like growth direction. Add a secondary highlight in the eyes using White + Raw Umber. Place Burnt Sienna + White in the corners of the eyes.

9 Place final highlights in the eyes, on top of the lightest area of lowlight, using White on a liner brush.

Begin basecoating the face, using dark areas of Raw Umber, rusty values of Burnt Sienna + Raw Sienna, as well as some straight Raw Sienna. Chop on colors with a no. 4 bright, following growth direction and observing the shorter hair length of the undercoat. Keep paint very sparse so it doesn't muddy when lighter values are added in the next step.

10 Once the undercoat is based in, you may begin to add the long, pale hair that characterizes this dog. These light areas may be wide and solid in some places, with fine, individual hairs laid on later. So don't think in terms of one hair at a time, but rather, use the no. 2 or 4 bright with enough brush pressure to create sections of hair. The mix should be Raw Sienna + White in a low enough value so that you still have plenty of room to move to lighter values when placing individual highlights on the hairs later.

Work carefully around the eyes, allowing the underlying shadows to set off the lighter overstrokes. Don't blend—just carefully apply the lights so they appear on top of the darker shadow areas of the color underneath.

11 Let the head area set up a bit while you begin basing in the various mixes on the body and legs. Base the ears with Raw Sienna, and Burnt Sienna + Raw Umber in darker value areas. Use Raw Sienna on the forehead, along with some of the Burnt Sienna + Raw Umber dark mix. Add shadows under the chin with Raw Umber and Raw Umber + Black. Lay on Raw Sienna on the paws, as well as some of the Burnt Sienna + Raw Umber mix for a darker value. Vary the sizes of brights you use to conform with the length of

hair and the size of area you are painting. Set up the growth direction now, in these early stages, by chopping on brush strokes with the chisel edge parallel to the lie of the hair. And don't use much paint: by minimizing the paint you apply to the surface, you'll be more effective in keeping the light hairs from getting muddy as you apply them in the next step.

12 Now comes the really fun part: creating the light values. Use Raw Sienna + White first, and gradually add a lighter value of White + Raw Sienna in the strongest highlight areas where needed. Take your time, and do *not* blend these light values into the darks below. They must be overlaid to give the impression of depth and shadow. After most of the lights are on, you might let the areas set up before attempting final lights.

13 Base the rest of the body with Raw Sienna in the darker value areas and Raw Sienna + White in the light values. Use chops of the chisel edge to get growth direction early on, but don't pull strokes for a hairy look. As the body recedes from the eye, the hair tends to look more dense and fluffy and less hairy. Also the hairs on the visible body are much shorter than those on the head and legs.

In addition, we want to keep the body pale, and allow it to recede into the background, to go away from us. Less detail will assist with that goal too.

14 Soften the values of the body hairs with short choppy brushstrokes where the values meet. Add a bit of shading for depth in front of the hind leg and on the back. Add any last highlights with a very pale value of White + Raw Sienna, chopping colors on with the growth. A very few guard hairs may be added to soften and to break up the outline shape of the animal with the same mix, slightly thinned with odorless thinner and applied with a liner brush.

Container

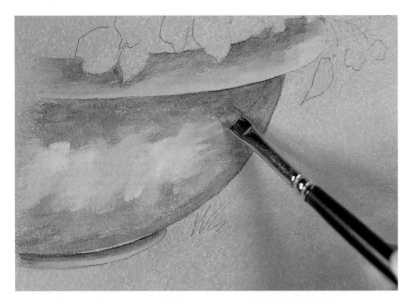

15 Base the container with a large bright using Raw Umber + Burnt Sienna for the darker value, Raw Sienna for mid-tones and Burnt Sienna + White for the lighter values. Lay colors on in broken lines, unevenly. That will make a soft blend easier to achieve.

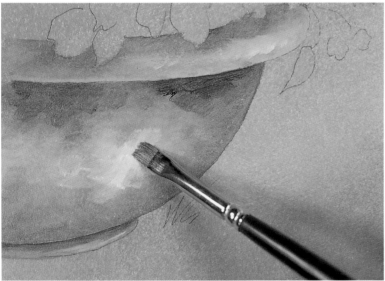

16 Using the largest bright, blend where values meet to create nice value gradations. A little splotchy surface texture is fine. Shade with Raw Umber in the darkest value areas, and highlight with White where strongest lights appear. The trick to perfect blending is this: sparse color at the basecoat stage, followed by dry applications of shading and highlights applied with firm pressure to the surface.

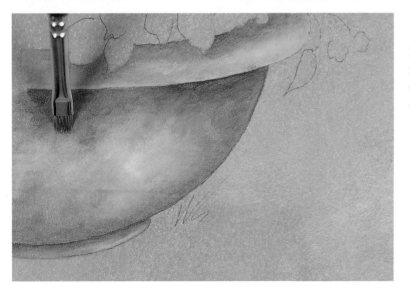

17 Blend the dark shading color where values meet. Do the same with the highlights. The final texture of the container is up to you: if you like a "painterly" look, as I do, simply don't blend the final lights and darks so smoothly.

Flowers

18 Fill in the darkest areas among the foliage in the container with Black + Sap Green. Base the dark values of the leaves and stems with Sap Green + Black, just a bit greener than the previous mix. Then base the light values in all the green areas using Sap Green + Raw Sienna + White. A no. 2 bright may work better for the tiniest areas, whereas a no. 4 bright will be just right for the larger leaf areas.

19 Using a dry chisel edge, blend with the growth direction of each leaf, pulling strokes from the edge toward the central vein, very, very close together. Highlight some leaves with a lighter value of the light green leaf mix. Add a stroke of the same value for some rolled edges on some leaves. Highlight stems with the light mix and add the veining on the leaves.

In this picture you can also see where I've allowed some of the dark green to smudge over into the edges of the sections where we'll add the alyssum. That is a nice way to give depth to the flower areas, and to keep every tiny blossom from appearing to be exactly the same value as its neighboring bloom.

20 Base the various flowers with these mixes:
Alyssum: White + Raw Sienna + Cadmium Yellow Pale.

Pinks: White + Purple Madder Alizarin + Raw Sienna. The centers
are white.

Pansy: Darkest values are sparse Purple Madder Alizarin. Light
value is Purple Madder Alizarin + Raw Sienna + White.

Violas: Darker values are Purple Madder Alizarin and Purple
Madder Alizarin + Raw Sienna. Lighter values are Cadmium Yellow
Pale + Raw Sienna. Use various small brights to make the mixes and
apply the colors sparsely.

21 *Alyssum:* Highlight a few more important blossoms with pure
White, using the no. 0 bright. Fill in the tiny centers with a
stroke of Black + Sap Green. Add four dots in a square with
Cadmium Yellow Pale.

Pinks: Add detail with a liner brush at the edges of the centers
using Alizarin Crimson. Add a few dots of Sap Green + Black at the
very center.

Pansy: Highlight the pink petals with white, blending with the
growth direction. Connect the dark values on the petal to the pink
areas by using the chisel edge to cut into the dark and pulling it out
just a bit here and there. Deepen within the original dark area using
Purple Madder Alizarin for the face. Add the detail for the tiny centers with a liner brush and Cadmium Yellow Pale for the center, and
White for the rolled petal edge.

Violas: Detail the yellow petals with fine lines of Purple Madder
Alizarin applied with the liner brush. Highlight the purple petals
along the edges with a little White + Raw Sienna, blended slightly
into the petal. Then, add centers with White, and a dot of Cadmium
Yellow Pale.

Final Steps

22 Lay in Black + Raw Umber shadows under the gosling with a small bright and unthinned paint.

Rough in the grassy areas with choppy strokes and slightly thinned Sap Green + Black. Lay some in front of the dog's feet, in front of the gosling, around the base of the container, and wherever else is needed for filler, and to give the idea that the area the animals are in is grassy, without getting too busy.

23 Using a pad of cheesecloth, soften the shadow under the gosling, and soften out most of the grasses you just painted, leaving "shadow" grasses for depth. Now using the same colors and method, come back and add grasses on top of the shadow grasses, pulling some up over the feet of the dog, in front of the gosling, and over the edge of the container. Use the leaf light value of Sap Green + Raw Sienna + White to highlight a few of the larger, more focal areas of grasses.

Add a few additional alyssum in front of the gosling to help balance the flowers in the container.

At this stage, you are also ready to add the final wet-on-dry highlights to the puppy and the gosling to bring out their forms and make them more interesting. You can see the strong unblended lights added here, some with Cadmium Yellow Pale + White on the gosling, and mostly White + Raw Sienna on the puppy. After I've established the pattern of lights as you see here, I'll begin to blend them, usually with the cheesecloth, to get the edges to soften nicely into the dry basecoat.

The very best thing about the addition of wet-on-dry highlights is this: it's a no-risk proposition. If you don't like them, you can simply use a little thinner and take them off again.

Gray Fox & Wood Rat

The beautiful gray fox is common in open woodlands and chaparral in all but the most northern of the mountain states. It's also one of our more common garden denizens. In areas where they are not persecuted, they become very tame and may be found searching for a lunchtime snack right outside your door. Besides being lovely to look at, they are greatly beneficial to the gardener because they are very skilled at chasing down even the most agile mouse.

Gray foxes also have a taste for fruit, and we treat ours to a Fig Newton or two when they come calling. One of their most unusual habits is that of climbing trees to escape from predators and perhaps also to search for unwary prey. They don't climb like a cat, but rather gracefully run up slanting tree trunks to walk along horizontal branches. I once saw one of "our" foxes some twenty feet up an oak tree.

Color Mixes

Use these swatches when mixing oils or matching to other paint mediums.

White + Raw Umber	Raw Umber + Black	Burnt Sienna + White	White + Raw Sienna + Sap Green	Raw Sienna + White

Alizarin Crimson + Purple Madder Alizarin + Raw Sienna	Burnt Sienna + Alizarin Crimson + White	Black + Raw Umber	Raw Umber + White	Black + Raw Umber + White

Black + Sap Green	Sap Green + Raw Sienna + White	Cadmium Yellow Pale + White	Raw Sienna + Raw Umber	Raw Sienna + Burnt Sienna

Line Drawing

Transfer this line drawing to the prepared
background using dark graphite paper. Be
very accurate when transferring the eyes and
facial features as well as the detail of the
flowers and the shape of the pot. Don't let
fur "grow" outside the drawing.

This pattern may be hand-traced or photocopied for personal use only. Enlarge at 157%
to bring it up to full size.

132

To paint the background, you'll need:

- Hardboard (Masonite) panel, 14" x 11" x ⅛" (36cm x 28cm x 3mm)
- Sponge rollers
- Acrylic paints by Delta Ceramcoat
  - Moss Green
  - Satchet Pink
  - Wild Rose
  - Seminole Green
  - Gamal Green
- Paper towels
- Protected work surface
- 320-grit wet/dry sandpaper
- Krylon Matte Finish no. 1311

To paint the Gray Fox and White-throated Wood Rat, you'll need:

- Oil paints
  - Ivory Black
  - Titanium White
  - Raw Sienna
  - Raw Umber
  - Burnt Sienna
  - Sap Green
  - Cadmium Yellow Pale
  - Alizarin Crimson
  - Purple Madder Alizarin
- Brushes
  - nos. 0, 2, 4, 6 and 8 red sable short brights
  - no. 0 red sable liner
- Odorless thinner
- Cobalt drier (optional)
- Palette knife
- Paper towels
- Disposable palette for oils
- Dark graphite paper
- Tracing paper
- Ballpoint pen
- Cheesecloth

Here's a helpful reference shot of one of our local foxes precariously-balanced on the top of an old wood fence. Many of us encourage these beautiful animals, so it's not unusual to see them in midday, offering an unusual and exciting photo opportunity. Notice the ticked salt-and-pepper areas of the coat that are varied with solid rufous areas. The cryptic colors of the coat are very close in hue to the surrounding dry-country landscape, giving the animal great protection.

PHOTO BY DEBORAH A. GALLOWAY

These attractive little mammals, with their large ears and soft gray coats, carry the official name of White-throated Wood Rat. But they are more affectionately known in the West as the Pack Rat for their unique behavior of piling sticks and debris as much as three feet (91cm) high over the entrance to their homes. This particular species adds spiny segments of cholla cactus to the lot, making it very discouraging for predators such as the fox.

PHOTO BY TERRY R. STEELE

Reference Photos & Eyes

We shoot flowers and containers of flowers at many nurseries and flower gardens, which are great resources for this kind of material. As you plan your photo, think about how you might use it. We find in our classes that many students can't resist shooting straight down into the flower, but that angle may offer little when you're ready to use the photo, especially if you wish to include other elements. It seems Deb is always kneeling or lying down in the grass (or dirt!) to get the perfect "mouse's eye" view of a floral element.

PHOTOS BY DEBORAH A. GALLOWAY

Looking Closely at Eyes

Base the eye colors precisely.

The brow casts shadows over the iris.

The highlight should fall within the iris.

The lowlight in the corner of the eye helps "seat" the eye in the head.

The highlight is placed on top of the strongest lowlight.

A few hairs pulled across the edge of the eye gives greater depth.

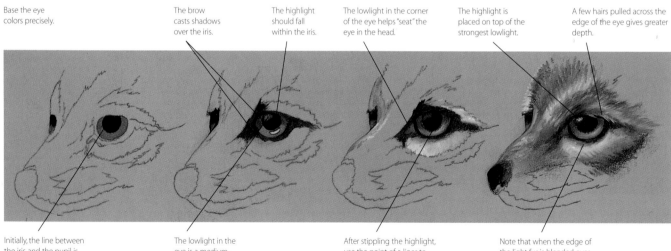

Initially, the line between the iris and the pupil is sharply defined.

The lowlight in the eye is a medium-value gray.

After stippling the highlight, use the point of a liner to "nick" the edges of the pupil and the iris to connect them.

Note that when the edge of the light fur is blended over the dark shadow, it gives roundness and dimension.

Background & Wood Rat

1 Review the background preparation instructions in chapter 2 before beginning.

Base the Masonite panel with Moss Green, using a sponge roller. Let dry and sand smooth. Then rebase with the same color, and, while wet, drizzle a little Sachet Pink and a little Wild Rose into the central area of the surface. Using the same sponge roller, blend these colors here and there, softening the edges to get a nice gradation into the light green background. Now drizzle a little Seminole Green in the corners of the surface and roll it splotchily into the surface, using a second roller. Then drizzle on some Gamal Green within the Seminole Green areas to deepen the colors, rolling to soften and blend. Finally, with the original roller, blend the edges of the greens to a smooth gradation. The background may remain a bit splotchy for an out-of-focus look behind the painting. Let dry and then sand again. Spray with Krylon Matte Finish no. 1311.

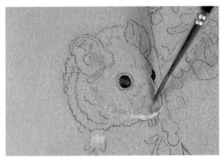

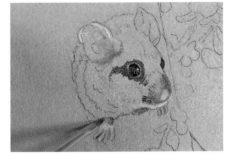

2 Base the toes, inside the ears, the nose and a little of the muzzle above the nose with Burnt Sienna + a tad of Alizarin Crimson + White using the no. 0 bright or no. 2 bright. Base the light area above the toes, as well as the chin with a little White. Shade a little around the nose with Burnt Sienna, using a liner brush.

Lay in the eye-ring using a liner brush and Raw Sienna + the Burnt Sienna mix used above. Wash the brush with thinner, blot it dry and then load in pure Black to base in the eyes.

3 Using the no. 0 bright, base around the eye with Black + Raw Umber, narrowing the eye-ring to a very fine line at the bottom of the eye. Leave it just slightly wider at the corners and above the eye. Using the liner brush, add the highlight dot with White in the near eye only.

Shade between the toes and on the leg, chin and nose with Raw Umber + Black using a no. 0 bright. Add a bit of White highlight on the nose.

Add a bit of Burnt Sienna shading at the bottom of both ears where they join the head. Using White + Raw Umber, add pale gray in the middle of the near ear. Then, outline the near ear with a lighter value of the same mix.

4 Highlight the toes with White + a little Burnt Sienna. Soften the shading on the leg into white. Add toenails with tiny strokes of Black, using the liner brush. Highlight the muzzle with White using the no. 0 bright.

Fill in the dark areas of the ears with Black + Raw Umber and the lighter value with White + Raw Umber on the far ear. Base the darkest areas of the body between the head and the pot with Black + Raw Umber.

Begin laying in the underlying dark values on the gray fur, using short choppy strokes of the no. 2 bright. Make the strongest shadow areas almost solid color.

Wood Rat & Flower Pot

5 Lay in the remainder of the Black + Raw Umber on the body. Notice how the color is more sparse in areas that will become lighter gray and denser in areas of shadow.

6 Using the no. 2 bright and perhaps, in tiniest areas, even the no. 0 bright, lay on the White + Raw Umber mix between the application of the darks. Chop your strokes in the same manner as you did for the dark value, following the growth direction and hair length. Next, use the same mix to highlight areas where more light is needed for contour. Finally, strengthen the darks inside the ears and rehighlight the edges of the near ear if needed.

7 Whiskers are done with the liner brush, using Black + Raw Umber, thinned with odorless thinner.

8 Begin by outlining the overhanging flowers and greenery with a very dark mix of Black + just a little Raw Umber, slightly thinned with odorless thinner, and applied with a liner brush. This method makes the basecoating much easier because you won't have to go into tiny crevices and corners with a larger brush. Then finish filling in the larger areas with the same mix, unthinned, on the no. 8 bright.

9 When the pot is based, eliminate brushstrokes, create a little uniform texture, and then lift a little paint in the highlight areas by patting the pot with a soft pad of cheesecloth.

Pot, Greenery & White Blossoms

10 Highlight the pot with splotchy areas of Black + Raw Umber + White, using the no. 8 bright.

11 Blend the highlights with the brush in smaller areas, and then soften with a cheesecloth in the larger, easier-to-reach areas.

12 Place small Black + Raw Umber shadows under the mouse, as well as under the feet and body of the pot, and soften the edges into the background using cheesecloth.

Place the dark value on all the leaves and stems with Black + Sap Green, using various sizes of brights for different sizes of leaves and stems.

13 Fill in the remaining areas of greenery with the light value of Sap Green + Raw Sienna + White. Blend where the values meet with the chisel edge of the brush and in the growth direction.

14 Place highlights on the leaves and stems using White + Sap Green + Raw Sienna. Blend a little where the values meet. Highlight in the centers of the larger leaves with a little White. Add any veining needed with the same light mix.

Add tiny white blossoms with strokes of the no. 0 or no. 2 bright, first with Raw Sienna + White and finally highlighting with a little straight White.

Petunias

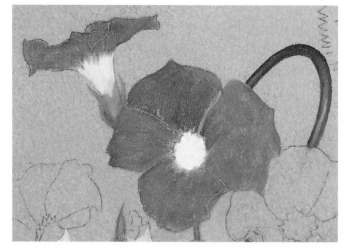

15 Base the petunia petals with Purple Madder Alizarin + Alizarin Crimson + Raw Sienna to dull and control the intensity of the mix. Base the center with White. Base the trumpet with Raw Sienna in the darker area and White in the lighter.

16 Blend between the values on the trumpet and where the trumpet meets the bases of the petals. Place the Sap Green + Black shading in the center. Blend the edges of the white centers into the base of each petal.

Divide the petals with dirty White veins. Then, using a no. 2 or no. 4 bright, place all the white highlights. Don't string highlights together so as to outline the petals. They should be placed naturally where light hits and bounces, as well as on petal overlaps to create depth.

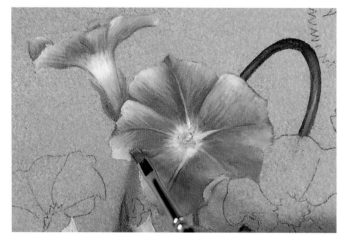

17 Blend the highlights using the chisel edge of the brush, and following the growth direction of the petals. Notice that the petunia petals each have a growth direction like that of a leaf, with the lateral (side) veins coming off the main vein. Pull from the edge of the petal toward the central vein as you work.

Add stamens in the flower centers with Cadmium Yellow Pale + Raw Sienna, and highlight with Cadmium Yellow Pale + White.

18 If some of the flowers seem too intense, dull them with a green mix of Sap Green + Black. The full, topmost flowers can be more intense, while the ones farther from the focal area and those set down farther in the container will be better balanced if they are duller.

Accent some of the larger leaves with the pinkish petal mix. Fill in the dark shadow areas within the pot with Black + Sap Green.

Finally, choose a few areas on the dominant blossoms on which to add final highlighting.

Fox

19 Base the iris of the fox's eye with Raw Sienna + Raw Umber. Shade at the top corners of the iris with Raw Umber, placing it on top of the basecoat. Place a narrow band of Black + Raw Umber around the iris, and shade at the corners of the eye with Black. Base the nose pad with Black. Base the chin and dark area on the muzzle with Black + Raw Umber.

20 Highlight within the iris at the bottom with Raw Sienna + White, using a no. 0 bright. Base the pupil with Black, using a no. 2 bright. Add a highlight with White. Add a little Burnt Sienna + White in the corner of the eye.

Place Raw Sienna in front of the dark on the muzzle, and White in front of that. Place a highlight on the nose with a grayed White.

21 Blend the first highlight in the eye slightly, and then rehighlight with a smaller, lighter dot of pure White. Blend the light in the iris slightly.

Tap with the chisel of a small bright between areas of color on the muzzle. Work the Raw Sienna into the dark behind and the white in front, in lines of texture. Blend the highlight on the nose pad and rehighlight if needed with additional, cleaner White.

Stipple White on the muzzle behind the nose with a liner brush.

22 Begin placing strong darks and areas of dominant color on the head and neck. Base the ears and ruff with Raw Sienna + Burnt Sienna. Place strong shadows in front of and under the eye with Burnt Sienna. Lay in Raw Umber + Black behind the eye, in the ears and at the gape of the mouth.

Fox, CONTINUED

23 Lay in the dark hair base under the ticking using short choppy strokes of a no. 4 bright loaded with Black + Raw Umber. Place strokes closer together and more densely in shadow areas and with a bit of space between them where grays will be lighter. Follow the growth direction of the head and neck carefully, and vary the stroke length according to the natural length of the hair in each area.

24 Now begin overlaying the white strokes to complete the salt-and-pepper ticking. Make from eight to ten strokes with a single dry brushload, and then reload out of a dry loading zone. Don't get impatient and place too much paint too quickly on the surface. That will only lead to mud.

25 When the head and neck ticking is complete and final lights have been added, use odorless thinner to thin a mix of Black + Raw Umber and place the whiskers with the liner brush.

26 Place solid areas of rufous color on the body and tail with a mix of Raw Sienna + a small amount of Burnt Sienna. Lay on all Black + Raw Umber base strokes in areas where hair is ticked. Where these color areas meet, walk the brush from one color to the next, chopping where values meet to connect them and make them appear part of the same animal. Change brush sizes to fit the hair length in each area, and follow the growth directions meticulously. Even with only the undercoat shown here, you can easily see the natural shape and contours of the fox's body and tail. Place Black + Raw Umber more densely in the areas of shadows and solidly along the median tail stripe.

27 Using the same brushes, pull out a loading zone of White, and use this light gray to begin filling in between all the dark strokes, blending a bit as you go, to create the light gray values that characterize the coat. This process will take a bit of time. Relax and work with the growth direction, and study the hair length in each area, so that the finished coat will look natural.

28 Add final highlights in areas of naturally stronger light, using first Raw Sienna + White, and finally a cleaner white applied with the same choppy strokes. These are the areas for emphasis: the top of the back, the front curve of the haunch, the gray and sienna ruffs on the chest, the middle of the front leg and the rufous stripe on the tail. Thin Raw Sienna + White with odorless thinner and place some guard hairs on the tail, the front of the haunch and the neck ruffs. Strengthen shadows at the curve of the hip and inside the front leg with unthinned Raw Umber. Make the black on the tail dense and dark if it appears too vague. Pull dark hairs from the central stripe on the tail over the adjacent areas.

When the fox is dry, use Raw Umber for shadows under the fox's tail. Blend these into the background with cheesecloth. See the final painting for reference.

Resources

Paints & Mediums

Delta Ceramcoat Acrylics:

DELTA TECHNICAL COATINGS, INC.
2550 Pellissier Place
Whittier, CA 90601
Phone: (800) 423-4135
Fax: (562) 695-5157
Web site: www.deltacrafts.com

Winsor & Newton Artists' Oil Colours:

COLART AMERICAS, INC.
11 Constitution Ave.
Piscataway, NJ 08855
Web site: www.winsornewton.com

Jo Sonja's Retarder & Antiquing Medium:

CHROMA, INC.
205 Bucky Drive
Lititz, PA 17543
Phone: (717) 626-8866
Web site: www.chroma-inc.com

Grumbacher Cobalt Drier:

SANFORD CORPORATION
2711 Washington Blvd.
Bellwood, IL 60104
Phone: (800) 323-0749
Web site: www.sanfordcorp.com

Brushes

WINSOR & NEWTON
ColArt Americas, Inc.
11 Constitution Ave.
Piscataway, NJ 08855
Web site: www.winsornewton.com

Canadian Retailers

CRAFTS CANADA
2745 29th St. N.E.
Calgary, AL, T1Y 7B5

FOLK ART ENTERPRISES
P.O. Box 1088
Ridgetown, ON, N0P 2C0
Tel: 888-214-0062

MACPHERSON CRAFT WHOLESALE
83 Quenn St. E.
P.O. Box 1870
St. Mary's, ON, N4X 1C2
Tel: 519-284-1741

MAUREEN MCNAUGHTON ENTERPRISES, INC.
RR #2
Belwood, ON, N0B 1J0
Tel: 519-843-5648
Fax: 519-843-6022
E-mail: maureen.mcnaughton.ent.inc@
sympatico.ca
Web site: www.maureen.mcnaughton.com

MERCURY ART & CRAFT SUPERSHOP
332 Wellington St.
London, ON, N6C 4P7
Tel: 519-434-1636

TOWN & COUNTRY FOLK ART SUPPLIES
93 Green Lane
Thornhill, ON, L3T 6K6
Tel: 905-882-0199

U.K. Retailers

ART EXPRESS
Index House
70 Burley Road
Leeds LS3 1JX
0800 731 4185
www.artexpress.co.uk

ATLANTIS ART MATERIALS
146 Brick Lane
London E1 6RU
020 7377 8855

CRAFTS WORLD (head office)
No. 8 North Street
Guildford
Surrey GU1 4 AF
07000 757070

GREEN & STONE
259 King's Road
London SW3 5EL
020 7352 0837

HOBBY CRAFTS (head office)
River Court
Southern Sector
Bournemouth International Airport
Christchurch
Dorset BH23 6SE
0800 272387

HOMECRAFTS DIRECT
PO Box 38
Leicester LE1 9BU
0116 251 3139

Index

The best in Decorative Painting instruction is from North Light Books!

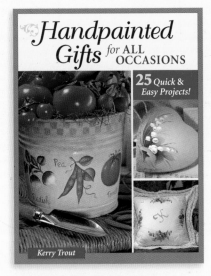

Create fabulous gifts and unique decor for holidays, family events and seasonal displays. You'll discover 29 easy to paint projects that are guided by step-by-step photos and straightforward instructions. Included are 12 "Quick Projects" that can be painted in an afternoon or less with inexpensive surfaces. Each project features a materials list, color swatch chart, and traceable patterns as well as colorful photos of the finished project.

ISBN 1-58180-426-1, paperback,
144 pages, #32590-K

Paint still life objects so realistic you'll want to reach out and touch them! You'll find complete, easy-to-follow instruction and proven techniques for painting realistic trompe l'oeil still lifes, florals and fruit. Mary McLean shares her unique approach to create three-dimensional forms with dramatically realistic results. Nine exciting projects make it easy to learn new techniques while painting everything from daffodils and apples to jelly jars and old-time crockery.

ISBN 1-58180-299-4, paperback,
128 pages, #32235-K

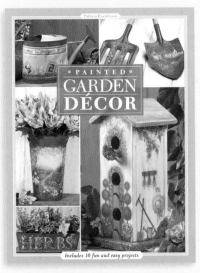

Add charm to your patio, porch or gazebo with *Painted Garden Décor*. Designer Patricia Eisenbraun provides step-by-step instructions and full color photos for lovely projects. You'll learn how to decorate a variety of pieces with peaceful scenes of outdoor life, flowers and other garden delights. Special patterns and worksheets ensure success, even if you've never painted before. You'll also find complete materials lists, preparation guidelines and basic brush stroke techniques.

ISBN 1-58180-460-1, paperback,
48 pages, #32717-K

Paint lovely flowers that transform baskets, boxes and more into elegant decorative pieces. Master Decorative Artist Sue Pruett illustrates techniques for painting floral details, from petals and stems to leaves and buds. Each gorgeous project includes a complete supply list, easy-to-follow patterns and step-by-step instructions—everything you need to get started and paint with confidence.

ISBN 1-58180-461-X, paperback,
48 pages, #32718-K

These books and other fine North Light titles are available from your local art & craft retailer, bookstore, online supplier or by calling 1-800-448-0915.